My Life in a
NUTSHELL

Life Is All About Fun, Frustration,
and Fulfillment

HANS STRICHOW

BALBOA
PRESS

A DIVISION OF HAY HOUSE

Balboa Press books may be ordered through booksellers or by contacting:

Balboa Press
A Division of Hay House
1663 Liberty Drive
Bloomington, IN 47403
www.balboapress.com
1 (877) 407-4847

Because of the dynamic nature of the Internet, any web addresses or links contained in this book may have changed since publication and may no longer be valid. The views expressed in this work are solely those of the author and do not necessarily reflect the views of the publisher, and the publisher hereby disclaims any responsibility for them.

The author of this book does not dispense medical advice or prescribe the use of any technique as a form of treatment for physical, emotional, or medical problems without the advice of a physician, either directly or indirectly. The intent of the author is only to offer information of a general nature to help you in your quest for emotional and spiritual well-being. In the event you use any of the information in this book for yourself, which is your constitutional right, the author and the publisher assume no responsibility for your actions.

Any people depicted in stock imagery provided by Thinkstock are models, and such images are being used for illustrative purposes only.
Certain stock imagery © Thinkstock.

Printed in the United States of America.

ISBN: 978-1-4525-1245-7 (sc)
ISBN: 978-1-4525-1244-0 (e)

Balboa Press rev. date: 12/11/2013

Contents

About the Front Page

Whilst our individual lives are played out in a myriad of fashions, each and every life is part of a bigger picture, 'Grand Order of Design', or Jigsaw Puzzle' that is ultimately associated with a universal cycle of life and death.

In that context, the title of this book and the image of 'My Life in a Nutshell' are designed to represent that cycle, which is essentially based on the need to break out of our shell and show the world who we really are.

And whilst this may require a sense of curiosity and pursuit of knowledge beyond our established comfort zone, or shell, this is 'Our Ultimate Purpose in Life', for which we have been predisposed by a higher power.

<u>Note</u>: The picture shows the author at 5 years old.

Introduction

Before I put pen to paper, I asked myself "What is there to tell about my life that could be of interest to any other person, from my family, friends and associates to the wider community, if not the world at large?"

The answer is obviously important, as my writings would have to be tailored to suit one or the other objective, if not all, unless I was simply out to please myself, in which case there would be no constraints.

As my personality traits and aspirations in life have always been goal oriented, I opted for the dream of becoming an author that could make it on the world stage for the simple reason that — "he had some to say".

So far so good, but what was it that I had say that could be of interest to anybody?

To put it in a "Nutshell", the answer lies with the one thing that combines the human race in the pursuit of a common goal, which can be put into three words: "Fun, Frustration and Fulfilment", it's as simple as that.

And whilst we begin our life with a clean slate, we are soon motivated to participate in the pursuit of a common goal on the premises that "Life is all about Fun", and so we apply ourselves to the best of our ability.

And then we grow up as we develop an attitude towards our family, friends, associates, the wider community, if not the world at large, based on a mixture of positive, passive and negative experiences and memories.

With that under our belt, we enter the second phase in the pursuit of a common goal as we are expected to fend for ourselves by getting out into the big wide world, when we find out that "Life is all about Frustration".

The phenomenon of life is reflected in the phrase that "Life is not meant to be easy", which was originally coined by George Bernard Shaw, the Irish dramatist & socialist (1856—1950) in his play "Back to Methuselah".

This brings me to my particular strengths and weaknesses as a contributor towards our common goal in the sense that every person is not only unique, but also equipped with a set of predetermined personality traits.

In the process, the world is made up of a) players in the game of life, and b) members of the audience, both of which are valid and honourable within the pursuit of a common goal, which brings me to 'my' predisposition.

That is, according to the experts who have studied the personality traits beyond our genetic predisposition and acquired skills and habits as a reflection of our upbringing, I am a 'player' in the game of life who is:

"Independent-minded, a thinker and a doer with little time for the established ways of doing things, unless they are personally tried and proven to fit a higher purpose, which cannot be explained or measured in real terms".

This would explain the frustration during my years of personal growth and development, and particularly my experiences in the businesses of industry, which tend to be driven by the adversities of their own making.

This takes us to the third phase where "Life is all about Fulfilment", in which case our sense of purpose is either based on our becoming a) a solution seeker, or b) a symptom bearer, both of which are honourable, once again.

In fact, it might surprise many of us to find out that there are no good guys and no bad guys, just solution seekers and symptom bearers, the significance of which can only be explained in the context of a common goal.

This reminds me of my busted eye and the surgeon who couldn't help herself questioning my sanity with words like "You people, why can't you be more careful", to which I replied "If it wasn't for people like me, you wouldn't have a job", which left her somewhat speechless.

At the same time, I am not advocating that we should purposely break the law or get into trouble for the sake of providing jobs, which may be a growth industry in some parts of the world, but has no future on the whole.

At this point, you may be curious about the proposition of a common goal for all mankind, or "Our Ultimate Purpose in Life", which has occupied the solution seekers for thousands of years without coming to an agreement.

That is, until now, as you will find out when you read my book entitled "Our Ultimate Purpose in Life", in which I have provided a science based connection between a "Grand Order of Design" and "The Human Condition".

In that context, this book is essentially an afterthought to the above mentioned book, as the possibility of my becoming a celebrated author could have been followed by a public demand for my autobiography.

Am I mad, do I have delusions of grandeur, or am I just expressing my fulfilment needs as a human being who has never shied away from a challenge, regardless of the great unknown and the seemingly impossible?

How can we tell the difference between the solution seekers and the symptom bearers, what are the points of reference, who determines these points, are we all mad and are we all going to die with the planet earth?

Well, I don't want to pre-empt my other book which has all the answers to the questions, and many more, and so I will embark on telling you all about "My Life in a Nutshell", as you are about to find out.

Part 1

LIFE IS ALL ABOUT "FUN"

I will start my story with my conception on a summer's day in early July 1940 in Germany in the town of Bremen, at a time when Hitler had invaded Poland and Britain and France declared war on Germany.

In a way, I have to thank 'Herr Hitler' for my being here simply because my father was given a break from fighting at the front, which led to his coming home and engaging in something entirely different, if you know what I mean.

At the same time, I was not supposed to have happened as I found out later when my mother confessed to me that I was an unplanned event that was nevertheless loved and raised with my older half sister, older brother and younger sister.

As it happened, I was born at home upstairs in the lounge room at number 58 Achterdiek in the suburb of Horn, Bremen, with the help of our local doctor and a neighbour, whilst my father was away at war in France.

With respect to my gestation, the war at the time did have its effects on me, the reality of which is partially reflected in my near death experience at the time of my birth, when the umbilical chord was wrapped many times around my neck.

1

My mother told me later that, every time a bomb went off, I did somersaults in the womb, which didn't do much for my supply of nutrients, yet I survived the experience without any obvious signs relating to the effects on my body.

This brings me to 'My Life in a Nutshell', which can be broken down into my childhood, adolescence, adulthood, parenthood and grandparenthood, each of which is portraying my traits as an *"Independent-minded thinker and a doer"*.

Ok, so I was born in the middle of World War 2, which seems to have affected me in some way, and I may never know the full extend of it, as I frequently ask myself "Why am I so obsessed with wanting to save the world?"

Surely, the same cannot be said for everybody that was ever born during a war, nor would it have to do with the fact that I was an Aries, in which case Adolf Hitler was an Aries and he was happily starting wars all over the place.

Actually, the answer didn't come to me until much later in life when I developed a theory relating to 'Our Ultimate Purpose in Life', the essence of which was associated with the mind and "The Process of Supernatural Selection".

That is, like the evolution of our body is associated with 'The Process of Natural Selection' and our survival on this planet, our mind is going through a similar process of evolution relating to our ultimate survival in the universe.

I even provided scientific evidence to that effect in my book, but I am only mentioning this as we are getting deeper into the mystery of my life and my idiosyncrasy as a 'Seeker of Eternal Life and Fulfilment', or 'SELF' for short.

I created the acronym of the 'SELF' in the context of 'Our Ultimate Purpose in Life' and the proposition that our real mission here on earth is:

"To pursue the great unknown so as to advance the human race, using the process of trial and error.

As a consequence, many problems are caused by people; however they are also solved by people.

The degree of our problems at any one time is proportionate to the perception of reality by one and all".

And whilst some people turn to God in their quest for eternal life and fulfilment, I was never very keen on any kind of believing, as I had *"little time for the established ways of doing things, unless they are personally tried and proven".*

As a consequence, whenever I was asked whether I believed in God, I would always say 'No', and when the response was somewhat horrified as in "How could you?" I would always reply that "I knew God personally and intimately."

I would then follow this up with an explanation of God being visible in the form of a 'Grand Order of Design' or 'GOD', after which I was generally left alone on the assumption that I was obviously a little bit weird and beyond help.

On that note, let me go back to my childhood and the fact that the war was raging all around us, and so we had to go to the bomb shelter on a regular basis and then witness the destruction on the way home, hoping there was a home to return to.

I remember on one occasion my mother was taking us to the shelter in a wooden cart when she suddenly remembered something she had to return home for, and so she left my brother and me wherever we happened to be at the time.

And as we laid back and looked towards the sky, we saw the allied bombers cruising above ready to discharge their deadly load onto the innocent victims below, which somehow never affected us, as we were too little to understand.

And to a large extent, the same applies to my upbringing and the periodical deprivation of my survival and safety needs, which didn't really sink in until much later when I looked back on what might have happened to me and my brother.

With respect to the deprivation of my basic needs, history has taught us that the health of a population during and after a war or time of restricted food supply tended to be better than its counterparts, as can be seen in the world of today.

However, I wasn't aware of this, nor would I have been interested in that finding when I was rummaging through the rubbish discarded by the occupying troops in the hope of finding something edible, like a half eaten sandwich or fruit.

At the same time, I am not apologizing for my becoming a thief on the odd occasion whenever the opportunity presented itself, like in summer and autumn when we stole fruit from the neighbours, some of which had orchards.

In fact, we acquired quite an art form as we organized ourselves with a lookout, a search party and finally a full-on attack on the strawberry patches, the plum trees, the apple trees, the peach trees and the berries, just to mention a few.

As to the latter, there were in fact a number of wild berry bushes which we frequented in late summer without having a full knowledge of the edibility of the berries, that is, until I inadvertently ate some nightshade berries.

And whilst there were no immediate effects, the symptoms of the poisonous berries were soon to become known as I kept falling asleep wherever I happened to be at the time, be it in the middle of the road or in some safer place of rest.

It wasn't until the next day that my parents became aware of this and the fact that we had been eating wild berries, and so I was rushed to hospital with a suspected case of poisoning which could have easily led to my death.

I don't know if the nurse hated my guts or whether it was hospital policy, but whenever I was violently sick and throwing up, the stupid woman forced me to eat my vomit until I was completely out of control and screaming my head off.

The good thing is that, after my release, I was sent to a farm in the country to recover from my ordeal, which I enjoyed thoroughly, especially for the fact that I was given plenty to eat and drink, which soon led to my full recovery.

This reminds me of my fourth birthday and the fact that I was given a loaf of bread, which I proceeded to devour there and then without sharing any of it with my family until I was bursting at the seam, which was about half way through the loaf.

It wasn't long after that the war finally came to an end on the 8th of May 1945, when Adolf Hitler had committed suicide and the allied troops were ready to return home, many of which were stationed in a Rhododendron Park near my home.

In fact, for a while I had to walk past a long line of army trucks and army personnel on my way to school at a time when many a soldier hadn't seen his family and kids for months and months, which worked in our favour.

That is, we were frequently beckoned to come and sit on their laps as they offered us chocolate and chewing gum, which we eagerly accepted as a sign of their good will and newly found peace amongst the nations.

Coming to the basic survival of the community at the time, each family was issued a coupon that could be exchanged for a quarter bucket of watered down turnip soup that might have filled our stomachs, but didn't really nourish us.

We were all running round with big bellies like you can see in some of the African nations, where the food shortages had affected the growth and development of the children more so than the adolescents and adults.

The value of money was also difficult to control as the inflation rate was often more than 100% per week, in which case you had to spend your wages immediately before they lost their purchasing power.

Instead of printing new notes, the government would overprint the existing notes with a higher value every week to the point where a pound of potatoes might cost two million dollars or more, that is, if they were available.

My father had returned from the war with a bullet through the knee, which healed reasonably well, whilst leaving him with one leg shorter than the other and a permanent limp that slowed him down to some extend.

When we asked him about the war, we would only receive some nominal information like when they raided a French farm house and he hid some jam jars under his jacket, when he accidentally fell running away.

According to him, his body was covered with strawberry jam from head to toe, which took him and his mates the next few days to lick from the clothing as they returned back to the front to fight the enemy in France.

On another occasion, he was referring to a tank attack where he was running away from an allied tank, when he fell into a bomb crater and the tank continued to run right over him without hurting him in any way.

He was also referring to the fact that his short stature came in handy as he could last longer on the same ration than his taller comrades, who tended to tire earlier and needed more rest to recuperate from the rigours of war.

On the whole, my father did not like to comment on any real war issues, and I guess he wanted to protect us from the incredible cruelty and deprivation associated with such an event on both sides of the divide.

school on the way home, when the trashcans were still untouched on the street.

One day, we found a packet of unopened condoms which we understood to be balloons that could easily be blown up and hung all over the house, which left my parents in a bit of a quandary when it came to their response.

Obviously, we were too young to understand the actual purpose of the condoms, and so they left us with the illusion of the balloon until we got tired of the whole thing and saw fit to discard them with some other rubbish.

Talking about discarded rubbish, the American troops had obviously left by then, and so there was no more chocolate and chewing gum, but there were other things of value left behind, like their weapons and ammunition.

To be specific, the troops that were near the road on my way to school had been picked up by the air force which was using the Autobahn near my home to land and take off, preferably without all the weaponry and ammunition.

And so the soldiers discarded them in the local creeks and ponds, where they slowly rotted away, that is, until we became aware of their existence and proceeded to retrieve them for personal and commercial reasons.

On a personal level, we emptied the powder from the ammunition and watched it light up the night whenever we started a fire to amuse us, which was sometimes bordering on the brink of sheer madness or suicide.

That is, somebody had the great idea to place a quantity of loaded cartridges into the fire and light it before watching them explode, whilst we were hiding behind trees until they were all done, which wasn't always the case.

On other occasions, we would retain the cartridge in a vice-like contraption and proceed to hit the back with a sharp object in the hope that the bullet would fly from the cartridge without blowing back into our faces.

Needless to say, there were a few close calls which our parents never got to hear about, yet there were many reports in the paper about kids of our age killing themselves or others, or having their hands blown off.

This brings me to the commercial reality of the metal or led associated with the bullets, and the brass associated with the cartridge, which we collected in large quantities before selling it to the scrap metal dealers.

We also found many handguns and rifles, which we tried to clean up and preserve as 'souvenirs' of the war, or sell on to dealers who were hoarding war time memorabilia in the hope that they would gain value.

In the process of doing all this, I had developed a liking for money, which led to my rummaging through the ruins in the nearby areas as well as the industrial area further away, which was flattened to the ground.

There was plenty of led piping, copper tubing and brass fittings that could be retrieved and converted into cash, if you had the desire to do so, which I did without hesitation and wholehearted support of my parents.

One day, we received a parcel from America which was entirely legal as it contained toys like bags of glass marbles, rubber balls, soft toys, lollies, miniature cars, picture books, bells and whistles and much more.

As for my part, I was happy to receive a blue rubber ball which I proceeded to share with my mates on the nearest open field, which turned into a massacre, as I was the only kid with a ball in the entire district.

That was until somebody kicked the ball into a huge blackberry bush that was bound to swallow up my precious ball forever, unless we were prepared to mow down the blackberries with whatever we could lay our hands on.

And mow down the blackberry bush we did, with the concerted effort of all my mates to the point where a professional mulching machine could not have done a better job, but to no avail, as there was no ball to be found.

Obviously, the temptation to steal the ball must have been too great for whoever found it, as it could not have vanished into thin air, yet the ball was never seen again in the entire district, like a stolen Rembrandt or Picasso.

Talk about vanishing, I felt like disappearing when my mother knitted me a pair of full length 'stockings' for winter from a multitude of coloured left over wool, simply because we couldn't afford full length trousers at the time.

I was the only kid at school with the latest fashion in winter wear, which might have been a hit with the girls, but the boys didn't appreciate that sort of thing, which they let me know in no uncertain terms.

When I was six years old, my parents got me a second hand ladies bike on my birthday, which I had trouble riding as the seat was too high for me, but that didn't stop me from getting around the neighbourhood.

That is, until my mate Werner came rushing out his garden with a big stick, which he proceeded to ram into the rear wheel of the bike to the point where the entire sequence of spokes had been torn from the rim.

And whilst I was generally known for my 'forgiving and forgetting' nature, this was too much even for me, and so I proceeded to approach his house and knock on the front door, when his mother answered.

As her husband was running an import business and the family had plenty of money, I had visions of getting a new bike, like any fair-minded person would do for an innocent victim like me, but I was in for a surprise.

That is, she took one look at me and exclaimed "Aren't you the boy who steals our plums, apples, cherries and strawberries? I have been meaning to talk to you!"

I guess we were even after that little incident, which left me without a bike, nevertheless, and so I started to save up for a brand new bike, one piece at a time beginning with the frame, which I then assembled in the attic.

Well, it took me a good six months of doing odd jobs like mowing lawns for the neighbours, delivering fish for the local fishmonger and groceries for the local grocer who remembered me from the 'no more credit' days.

And then the moment came when the bike was finished in all its glory, upon which I was the envy of the boys in the neighbourhood who were basically waiting for their parents to buy them everything they wanted.

For me, this was not a reliable process of acquisition, which might have had to do with my preconditioning as an Aries who *"must be absolutely occupied, where nothing is more horrible than an idle moment, as it throws itself into activities only to pass time"*.

This became obvious when I spent my time delivering fish on Saturday's rather than playing with my mates, whereby the deliveries were made with the use of a heavy duty bike with a huge basket in the front.

On some occasions, I would have to climb many stairs as the customer might have lived in a high rise building up to ten stories high, in which case my bike and the remaining fish was left unattended in the street below.

Strangely enough, nobody ever stole any of my fish, which was a blessing as I would have had to pay for the damage, which is probably the reason why the potential thief might have decided not exploit the opportunity.

On one of my rounds, I would have to ride down a long driveway to a farmhouse which was protected by a vicious German-Shepherd dog and an equally vicious Doberman, who usually greeted me right at the street.

In order to protect myself, I would peddle with one leg whilst the other leg was positioned on the cross bar, which worked out fine until I had a dog on either side, in which case I had to try and outrun the dogs with my bike.

Fortunately, the farmer's wife appreciated my gallant delivery of fish as she handed my a tip that was worth the odd bite, not to mention the occasional torn trousers which my mother always managed to repair, by hand.

On another occasion, I would deliver fish to a lady in a wheelchair in a big house, where she was all by herself and visibly distraught by her condition and the fact that nobody ever came to visit her, except for me on occasions.

I took a liking to the old lady as she told me about her life on the stage and the accident that took her away from her profession as an artist and exposure to a life audience, which obviously had affected her state of mind.

Apart from the fact that she always gave me a generous tip, I sometimes visited her on my way home when I made her a cup of tea and we chatted about life in general and possibly my brilliant career that was yet to unfold.

At the end of my deliveries, I would have to add up the takings and reconcile the amount with the boss, which always worked out OK, except for this one day when I was short by 20 DM, (Deutsch Mark) which was a lot of money at the time.

In my frustration, I revisited every household in the hope that I had given somebody 20 DM too much change, as in one note in paper money, but there was no such luck, and so I returned to the shop empty handed.

And whilst the shopkeeper didn't exactly accuse me of stealing, he nevertheless felt that he had to teach me a lesson, which he did by deducting 5 DM from my wages over the next few weeks, which left me with nothing.

I was quite upset when I got home that day and the week thereafter, which prompted my mother to visit the fish monger so as to inform him of my mental anguish and the obvious fact that I hadn't stolen the money.

Low and behold, the fishmonger informed me the next Saturday that I had learnt my lesson, and so he released me from having to pay the last 10 DM, which made me really happy as I continued to work for him.

Some of my work included the sweeping of the yard and unfolding of old newspapers which were used to wrap the fish, which I did in the cellar where all the packing material was kept, as well as the walk-in freezer.

I must confess, the temptation was too much for me whenever I had to go into the freezer for one thing or another, as there was a smorgasbord of delicacies like shrimps in mayonnaise, crab salad, herring salad and many more.

I just took hands full of the best there was, which I devoured there and then with a subconscious motivation for food that goes right back to the war years and my scavenging for left over bits of sandwich or fruit.

Even to this day, I can't control this urge whenever I am confronted with food, which isn't helped much by the fact that my beautiful wife of 48 years is one hell of a good cook, which is only one of her many talents.

Now, before you come to the conclusion that I didn't have any fun in my youth, let me assure you that this is not the case, as you will discover when I tell you about my collecting birds eggs, feathers, rocks, stamps and butterflies, just to mention a few.

The latter brings back memories of catching butterflies with a homemade net, after which we would place a drop of Ether on the head which killed them painlessly, before we pinned them to a board and opened their wings.

We knew all the names of the butterflies, the most precious of which was the 'Swallowtail', which only appeared here and there without ever being caught, with the exception of this one time, which I am sorry to tell you about.

That is, there was a bunch of us looking out for something fluttering by, when somebody yelled out "Swallowtail", upon which we all raced to the place where the mysterious sighting had taken place, and fair enough – there it was.

You can imagine half a dozen mad dogs chasing after one little butterfly, pushing and shoving each other out of the way for the privilege of being the one and only who had ever caught the catch of them all.

As it happened, we all converged on the poor creature as it settled on a bush, upon which we all smashed our nets in unison on the fragile critter to the point where there was frightfully little left of it, such are the horrors of hunting.

Whatever butterflies we caught were placed in a cigar box on cotton wool which was then covered with a piece of glass held down with masking tape and hung on the wall of my little space in the only bedroom which I shared with my brother and sister.

My parents were sleeping in the sitting room on a convertible couch, which was restored every morning after we had breakfast in a tiny kitchen with a sloping ceiling that was further reducing the available space.

And all of this was positioned in the second storey of an attached housing estate that was designed to accommodate 2 families (side by side) under normal circumstances, but accommodated 4 when we lived there.

The people below us had 2 girls and a boy who was about my age and learning the guitar, which he was doing one note at a time, which was driving us mad as he played the note 'C' for 10 minutes and then the 'D' note etc.

Since we didn't have a shower or a bathroom, my mother would set up a steel tub on two chairs which she filled with warm water for me and my brother so that we may get our once a fortnight debugging and general clean up.

You can guess what comes next insomuch that my brother and I had a good old punch up in the tub until we ended up on the floor, tub and all, whilst the water spilled all over the kitchen and through the floor into the downstairs kitchen.

As far as I was concerned, this made up for the guitar torture, but the downstairs neighbour didn't see it that way, as they refused to talk to us for some time to come.

And then the neighbour diagonally from us as in next door downstairs got himself a television, which he turned up to a level that was unhealthy to the normal ear, even when you lived as far as next door and upstairs.

You can imagine my father who had a short fuse at the best of times, which began with his banging the walls until the noise subsided for a minute or two, before it went up even higher.

Well, this somehow inspired my father to invent a TV combating device consisting of an electric shaver that had its 'interference controller' removed, upon which the TV picture would come out all fuzzy and distorted.

And whilst this did the trick, it did nothing for the relationship between our family and the rest of the block, which was further aggravated by the fact that we didn't have a proper toilet.

Instead, we had a little walk-in cupboard which we used as a toilet by way of a bucket in a box with a lid, the emptying of which had fallen into my lap after my brother left home at the age of 15, when he went to sea.

His reason for doing so was based on the fact that my father had a terrible temper as he frequently threatened to kill the lot of us, whilst throwing plates of hot soup against the wall, before storming off in a mood.

There were many times when we were huddled in a corner with the imminent threat of death over our head, but somehow it never came to that, which was nevertheless the reason why my brother left home prematurely.

Coming back to my responsibility for emptying the shit-bucket, I usually waited until it was full to the rim, upon which I would lift it out of the box and carry it down the stairs with the odd little spillage here and there.

Well, you can imagine the smell of the stairway, not to mention the beating I got from my father, which didn't endear me to his ways of raising a loving family, but what could I do, as I was too young to leave home.

Anyway, another neighbour decided one day to grow asparagus, for which he had created a number of garden beds which he cared for with love and the best fertilizer you could get at the time – the shit in our pit.

That is, when I came home from school one day, there was a tanker pumping our shit straight onto the neighbour's garden beds, which might have been good for the plants, but it didn't do much for the atmosphere.

Needless to say, we weren't popular for allowing our shit to be used for such a purpose, the smell of which lingered for weeks, and even the promise of a free bunch of asparagus couldn't make up for that.

By all accounts, we were still relatively poor to the point where I was told that we couldn't afford a second house key, which was normally held by my mother who wasn't necessarily at home when I cam back from school.

Being a survivor and basically self-sufficient by nature, I soon came up with my own version of a key in the form a bent wire that could be used to open virtually any front door with a bit of wriggling and fiddling.

My father seemed to be getting on top of his game as a camera man and photographer when he started to make documentaries and animated films, which covered a variety of subjects, including a large bakery.

You should have seen our faces one night when he came home with trays and trays of 'sample' cream cakes and other delicious goodies, which was basically too much for us, and so we asked the neighbours to join us.

It is amazing what a little bit of goodwill can do for all the bitterness that had developed in the past, as you can see in the 'forgiving and forgetting' that went on at the time, not to mention the usual flow of alcohol.

In those days, we couldn't buy milk at the grocery in sealed containers, as it was delivered to your house by a milkman with a bell and a truck with a tank full of un-pasteurised and un-homogenized milk straight from the cow.

We would take our milk bucket and get it filled with a litre or two before putting it on the windowsill to keep cool, as we didn't have a fridge in those days, which also meant that we had to use it within 24 hours.

In summer, one of the ways of using the milk was to pour it into a number of plates, then spit into it before placing it in a humid area like the attic or similar warm place so as to facilitate the fermentation process over night.

In the morning, we would have the best yoghurt under the sun, with a thick layer of cream on the top which, together with a bit of sugar or honey, was a meal fit for a king.

Now that there was a little money coming in, we were actually getting new clothes like 'Lederhosen' or short leather pants which we wore all through the summer to the point where they had taken on a permanent shape.

In fact, they felt more like a fixed armour than a piece of clothing, which often led to a rash on our legs due to the constant rubbing – so much for the traditional way of dressing, which was often not designed for comfort.

My father even bought a second hand Volkswagen beetle with a split rear window, 6 Volt battery, 1.2 litre engine and cable brakes, all of which might add up to 80 km per hour on a sunny day with the wind from behind.

Not to be outdone, our TV neighbour bought himself a second hand Ford that didn't have a starter motor, but this didn't seem to worry him as he relied on all of us every morning to push start him down the road.

The upside of all this lies in the simple fact that we didn't need Gyms or exercise gadgets in those days, as Mother Nature had bestowed us with a sufficient number of daily chores and challenges for 'Freeeee'.

I remember one summer we were holidaying on a farm in the country, where my brother and I got friendly with the local boys who were keen to show us their creations like a tree house and an underground cave.

The tree house was a good 50 feet in the air in an old pine tree that was basically out of sight and inaccessible unless you knew the hidden ropes that led to the hidden lift which was operated by a system of pulleys.

They told us that, if there was another war and we would be taken over by another force, they could live in the tree house for ever, which was further substantiated by the spacious underground man made cave.

The cave was virtually impossible to trace as there was a small trap door with natural growth on it that led you down a tunnel into a roomy cave with beds, storage facilities and electrical lighting from a nearby waterwheel.

That was quite an eye opener for us city kids, which brings me to the next day when it was Poppy harvesting and we were invited to help with the picking and loading onto a horse and cart, which was then taken to the farm.

That evening, my brother and I got up on the wooden cart and proceeded to gorge ourselves on the poppy seeds, which came straight from the fruit together with the opium covering the black/blue seeds. (This is usually washed off when sold)

After a while, we were quite full and feeling a little woozy as we lay under the cart to have a little rest, which turned out to be more of an opium trip into an unknown world of amazement and magic than a simply nap.

Fortunately for us, our parents never found out about our little 'experiment' with drugs, which is just as well, as we would have really copped the full force of my father's long and vicious arm of the law, or punishment.

Apart from all the fun we had in the summer, we also had our special activities in autumn, one of which was the gathering of acorns which we then sold to the local pig farmer who used them to feed the pigs in winter.

One year, there was a particularly good season to the point where the farmer had more than enough for the coming winter, and so we returned home with our harvest and proceeded to throw them at each other, which was great fun.

Other than that, we would pick horse chestnuts which we converted into necklaces, hazelnuts which were growing wild in the area, elderberries which my mother turned into elderberry juice, and catch fish in the creeks.

The latter was based on a couple of popular methods, one of which was to tie a thin copper wire to a long stick with a sling at the end of the wire, which was then lowered down into the water and over the head of a pike. (fish)

The pike had a habit of sitting still in the flowing water whilst waiting for smaller prey, which lent itself perfectly for this type of fishing, which was nevertheless not as exciting as hunting the pike with a bow and arrow.

All the kids in the neighbourhood had a bow made from bamboo and arrows made from tree branches together with feather quill at the end, which we aimed somewhat below the pike so as to accommodate the optic distortion.

Imagine the excitement when we hit the pike and it took off with the arrow going through the water until it tired and we could lift it out of the water to finish it off, before we sold it to the local fishmonger or took it home to Mum.

At this point, I must explain the countryside around my hometown in north Germany, which was flat as a pancake and criss-crossed with little canals and creeks that were basically designed to get rid of the excess water.

The whole scene was a bit like Holland, where the North Sea was often higher than the land and regularly flooded if it hadn't been for the dykes and the canals and the lochs that were used to manage the flow of water.

In the case of my best mate Klaus and his father's property which was near to my home, the canal was feeding into a long small tunnel under his property which was frequently blocked with debris and tree branches.

We were standing near the entry of the tunnel on one of these occasions when it was almost closed completely, with the exception of six inches or so at the top, when Klaus's father came along and issued a challenge.

That is, he offered 10 DM to anybody who had the guts to climb into the tunnel and push the debris all the way through to the other side so that the flow of water would be restored for another year or so, and guess what?

Without hesitation, I stripped off there and then as I climbed into the icy cold water and proceeded to push the muck and the debris through to the other side, whilst I kept an eye on the rats that were running back and forth in front of me.

I can still hear the applause when I surfaced on the other side, not realizing that these types of tunnels are frequently filled with poisonous gases that would have killed me if it hadn't been for my lucky stars.

Whilst we are on the subject of killing, I remember this one day when we had erected a kind of dartboard which we used as target practice for our homemade three-pronged spears, as in three pointed steel nails set in a long stick.

And just when I was retrieving my spear and turned around, this bloody idiot decided to throw his spear, which entered my face just below the right eye, much to the amusement of all the other bloody idiots around me.

Well, what could I do but laugh off the whole thing, whilst the blood was running down my face, and there was no-one there to give me a Tetanus shot for the three rusty nails, none of which ever got back to my parents.

We also smoked pipes which we carved from the wood of a Linden tree, whereby the hole through the long mouth piece was made with a red hot knitting needle, after which we loaded the pipe with dry leaves and herbs.

And when the winds arrived in autumn, we would make kites which we flew high up in the air to the point where we could barely see them, whilst we sent messages up the string in the form of a sail-like folded piece of paper.

The fun went on and on as we made blow pipes from the hollow branches of the Elderberry tree, which we then used to fire the ripe berries of the Birdberry tree, which left a nice red mark on our clothing and body.

Another autumn fun activity was the burning of the dry dead grass in the bushland, which we did every year to the point where we had burnt hair and eyebrows whenever we had to distinguish some of the fires before they got out of control.

Needless to day, we stunk like nothing on earth, but my mother never complained, which brings me to another little fire experience when we were sitting around a camp fire in my best mate's back yard, where I was shielding my face with my hands.

My best mate's father was a master painter and he had a number of painters working for him, one of which was a loudmouth no good for nothing apprentice who thought he might do us a favour by pouring thinner on the fire.

Just as well I had my hands in front of my face, as I was the closest to the fire with short trousers and bare legs in a crouched position, because I received severe burns to both of my legs, which put me out of action for a while.

I was in bed for three weeks as I watched my legs blister up and slowly heal, during which I never complained and never shed a tear, despite the incredible pain associated with the ordeal—I was becoming a man.

As my best mate was now starting to work for his father and I was still at school, I was the head of the little gang roaming the area when we came across another mob that was challenging us to a fight.

The leader of the mob was about twice my size and also older, which didn't perturb me as we discussed the particular method of fighting, in which case I opted for wrestling, considering he had an advantage in boxing.

I had no idea when it came to wrestling other than the odd friendly fight with my mates, which came in handy as I managed to get him on the ground before placing him into a headlock which he was unable to get out of.

To be honest, I was shit scared as I considered my fate when he eventually got out, and so I tightened my grip even further whilst I assured him that I meant him no harm and I was just lucky to land him the way I did.

As he lay there helplessly, I offered to let him go, but he refused as he claimed he would be able to get out of the situation, after which he would beat the living daylight out of me, and so we laid there for another 20 minutes or so.

Well, the boys were getting rather bored with all this passive fighting, and so they decided to set fire to the grass around us, which proceeded to engulf us to the point where we had to get up if only to safe our lives.

It wasn't long after that when my brother and I were looking for adventure in the nearby Rhododendron Park, and so we decided to climb this huge oak tree all the way to the top, where we could hardly be seen.

And just when we were almost out of sight, this park inspector came along and discovered us in the tree, upon which he shouted and swore at us just in time for my parents who were going for a stroll in the park.

Isn't it terrible, they exclaimed to the inspector, you would think their parents would have better control over them, to which the inspector agreed as they left us at the top of the tree without being any wiser.

That night when we got home, my mother was telling us about these terrible children that were allowed to roam free and climb trees, to which we nodded knowingly and sympathetically without moving a muscle.

Apart from the trees, we also had a lot of fun mastering the canals and creeks in the area, for which we had developed a kind of art form that would allow us to get from one side to the other without having to go to the nearest bridge.

One such way was to use a long pole that could be placed in the middle of a creek and then used as a means of running and jumping onto the pole in the hope that it would have sufficient momentum to get us to the other side.

And whilst in the majority of cases the method worked in our favour, on the odd occasion the pole would either go to the halfway mark and then sidewards, or it was simply too short to get us to the other side.

On other occasions, there might have been a smallish and seemingly flexible tree right at the edge of the creek, and you know exactly what was going through our mind at the time, as you too would climb the tree and use it to lower yourself on the other side, wouldn't you?

In doing so, you would have experienced the excitement associated with the tree breaking right on the halfway mark, after which you would have been too busy saving yourself than to think about how silly you are.

This takes me to the odd large tree with a strong branch right over the creek, to which we would attach a rope so that we could swing ourselves across like Tarzan in the jungle, which is not as easy at it sounds.

That is, it would take some learning when it came to the right moment to let go of the rope, and if you missed, you either fell into the creek, or you hung there until kingdom come or you just fell into the creek, whichever came first.

Finally, there was always the straight forward 'run and jump' method of crossing a creek, in which case you had to know your distance which was based on the process of trial and error, once again—such is life.

Talk about how silly one can get, we were very good at this sort of thing as we saw fit to annoy the hell out of the local wasp population whenever we found their nests in one the tree trunks in the area.

That is, apart from throwing rocks and mud at the opening of the nest, some of us were stupid enough to poke sticks into the nest, after which a swarm of wasps or hornets would attack us until we withdrew ourselves.

At the same time, we would have had enough bites and toxins in our blood to last us for the whole year, that is, until it was time to annoy the little critters once again, such was the nature of our stupidity.

On a warm day, we would go to the local open air swimming pool which was dug directly into the peat like ground and bordered with concrete edges, whilst a two storey diving tower had been erected directly in the centre.

We would watch the older boys diving from both levels, many of which ended up with a bellyflop or some other unplanned outcome that sometimes led to a fatal situation, if nobody had been watching at the time.

Some of this had to do with the fact that the water was a murky dark brown tea like colour derived from the moors in the area, which didn't allow you any kind of vision whatsoever.

Hence, if somebody didn't surface after a dive gone wrong, we would either dash all the way around the pool to inform the supervisor of the fact, or the person would just disappear without any notification.

If and when the supervisor did get notified, he and a few other qualified lifesavers would be diving in and around the last area of observation, which sometimes led to the recovery of the person – dead or alive.

If not, the pool would be closed down and a rowing boat was deployed together with a dragnet that was systematically searching the pool until the body was found, which was always great 'fun' to watch.

One time, we were sitting on a dam-like hill next to the pool watching the big boys doing their stuff to impress the girls, one of which was to dive to the bottom of the pool and bring up fist size life mussels, which was forbidden.

And whilst this was often observed directly by the supervisor who threatened to remove the offenders from the pool, this only seemed to impress the girls even more so, and to think that 'we' thought we were stupid.

As to our affection for the girls, I remember this boy holding his girlfriend by the hands as he gently pulled her face to face out of the pool, when suddenly her bathers slipped below her 'big' breasts, which we applauded in unison.

On another occasion, I decided to visit my grandparents in Harburg near Hamburg this particular holiday when I was about 12 years old, which involved a bicycle trip of some 100 kilometres, no sweat.

There were no real safety concerns in those days, as I was setting off in the morning and arrived at my grandparents in the afternoon, the latter of which was not communicated to my parents as we didn't have a phone.

Anyway, the next day my grandfather asked me if I wanted to help him with his casual job in a cheese cellar, to which I agreed without having any idea with respect to what was involved and whether I could do the work.

The place was not far from where he lived, and so we walked to the cellar and opened the door and I was hit by a wall of Ammonia fumes which was so strong and overwhelming that I refused to enter at first.

After a while, my conscience got the better of me as I agreed to help him with the periodical cleaning and reversing of the huge circular cheeses, which were stacked four per tray up to the ceiling on wooden racks.

The Ammonia smell came from the washing medium consisting of diluted Ammonia and salt that was used to wash the cheeses twice a year until they were ready to be sold, by which time they were worth a pretty penny.

The premises were 'controlled' by a vicious German-Shepherd dog which was normally on a chain, which was just as well, as he growled at me with a snarling action whilst showing me his huge teeth in the process.

I soon discovered that the dog had developed a liking for cheese, which I exploited on a daily basis by giving him some of the reject cheese until he was eating out of my hand and we became the best of buddies.

The dog was not the only one that had developed a taste for smelly cheese, as I found out later in life when the smell of a ripe to overripe cheese was really turning me on, like the smell of the 'Harzer' and 'Limburger' cheese.

Some of this had to do with the fact that my grandfather was allowed to take home as much overripe cheese as he could carry, some of which he gave to the neighbours and some of which was devoured by us at home.

On Saturday, my grandmother would take me to the market where my uncle on my father's side had a delicatessen shop, where we 'inherited' some ham, cheese, butter, a variety of 'Wursts' and other delicacies.

And then it was time to return home, as I carried my bike down the stairs and said goodbye to my grandparents with my saddlebags loaded with goodies that left a trail of overripe cheese all the way back home to Bremen.

I soon reunited with my mates, when we decided one night to break loose and take the rout to a given destination by jumping fences and crossing backyards as the crow flies in the hope that we wouldn't come across any vicious dogs.

And whilst our wish was granted on that score, we did come across a railway line just when a train was rattling past, when one of my mates picked up a rock and threw it at the train, something we all lived to regret.

Before I come to that, let me continue with our night of terror as we entered an unknown street, when one of my mates issued a challenge that was too tempting for a dickhead like me, as you are about to find out.

That is, he dared me to climb the nearest lamp post right to the top, after which I would be his hero of the moment, which was enough motivation for me as I climbed the lamp post and unscrewed the globe in the process.

If that wasn't enough, he dared me to do the same thing again and again, which I did with a determination that was boarding on sheer madness, but this was the furthest thing on my mind, as I proceeded with my task.

As it happened, the street was a dead end which I didn't realize until I slid down the 'last post' and right into the arms of one of the residents who had witnessed the gradual dimming of the lights and decided to make a citizen's arrest.

Unfortunately, I was not the only one getting caught, yet a couple of my mates got away, including my best mate Klaus who pleaded with me thereafter not to give him away, which I didn't regardless of the pressure from the police.

This brings me back to the rock and the train in the sense that the police were questioning us with respect to our whereabouts at the time of the train incident, which they traced back to the spot where we were at the time.

We were told that the rock had broken a window and just missed a passenger, which was duly reported to the police who then established the location which led to their suspicion with respect to our whereabouts at the time.

Well, the beans got spilled and I was sent to a juvenile prison for two weekends in a row, whilst the silly bugger who threw the rock got four weeks, whereas Klaus got away Scott free, the lucky bastard.

I must confess, I had the best time ever when I went to jail on Saturday and overnight to Sunday, partially due to the acoustic being the best I had ever come across, that is, until the jail warden got hold of me.

To be specific, I was lying on my back in this empty room surrounded by bare bluestone with a bucket in one corner and a bed, a table and a chair in the other, when I began to yell out my favourite Rock and Roll songs.

Well, that didn't do much for the warden as he proceeded to hammer on the door so as to shut me up with threats of throwing me into some dark dungeon which would scare the living daylight out of me.

That seemed to settle me down as I surveyed the rest of the room and pulled myself up to the window to see the long term holiday makers having their daily bit of exercise in the yard, which was all very satisfactory.

From hereon, I was given the full weekender treatment as I received courteous and prompt room service offering me a variety of refreshments from clean tap water to black coffee or tea, together with a piece of black bread.

And then the door opened and the local priest walked in, which I had never encountered in my life so far as a Heathen, which he seemed to take on as a bit of a challenge as he proceeded to inform me of the love of God.

He then requested that I was to write an essay about my sins and to forward that essay to him the next morning so that we could work out a plan for my salvation, talk about a laugh a minute in jail, where I least expected it.

I could hardly wait to get back to jail the next weekend, wondering what they had installed for me this time round, and I was not disappointed as I experienced another day of excitement and entertainment at the government's expense.

I quickly settled back into my normal routine of stealing from the bakery when the baker's wife left the shop because we were inquiring about something that was obviously not on display, which was all part of the plan.

Another routine had to do with the local paper and magazine stand which, apart from a variety of sweets and drinks, was selling our favourite Cowboy and Indians paperbacks which came out with a new edition every week.

As to the well rehearsed routine, one of us would distract the lady whilst the other slipped a copy of the latest issue under his jumper before walking away with the innocence of a child that couldn't do wrong if it tried.

That night under a blanket with a torch, I would read the story about Billy Jenkins shooting the crap out of some Indians and cattle wrestlers, as he was the fastest gun in the West and nobody dared to disprove him.

Before I move on, let me tell you a little about my family starting with my father who, as you know already, was a little strange to say the least, some of which had to do with the fact that he was very clever and easily frustrated.

This became obvious when he invented the first 'silent movie camera housing' which allowed him to get close to some wildlife without having the whirring of the camera getting in the way and frighten the birds and other wildlife.

Mind you, there was a bit of a drama along the way as my father developed the contraption in the attic, using plaster of Paris as the primary source of material for the housing of the movie camera, which was obviously hidden inside.

And just when he was about to finish his marvellous invention, he dropped the bloody thing on the ground, upon which it disintegrated into a pile of rubble that left my father foaming at the mouth, whilst we fled from the scene of the accident.

Another day in summer, my parents invited a favourite uncle and aunt of mine to our (little shit) house, where they sat in the garden and admired the beautiful flowers which my parents had planted with love and devotion.

My uncle had a good sense of humour, and he must have thought the same of my father as he calmly declared that "You know Karl, if you didn't have this beautiful garden, we would have never visited you".

Well, if you think the atom bomb left its mark, you don't know my father as he promptly exploded with an instant fuse before he disposed of my uncle and aunt with a serious of swear words I had never heard before.

OK, one down and two more to go, as I found out when my grandfather and grandmother on my mother's side showed up one day with presents for the kids, compliments for my mother and their daughter, and contempt for my father.

An again, the happy reunion came to a quick end as my father sent them on their way and told them not to come back, after which we were barred from seeing my grandparents, which we hitherto ignored, like so many of his instructions.

From thereon, nobody dared to come close to us, which didn't really bother us kids as we were too busy doing our own thing, especially in winter when the weather was cold enough to freeze the creeks and canals.

Under the circumstances, the thickness of the ice was always a bit tricky when it came to its adequacy for holding our bodily weight, in which case I was given the role of test pilot because I was of a relatively small statue.

The rule was simple insomuch that, if I fell through the ice, the thickness would not yet be ready for general consumption, and so it went on and on until I returned in one piece and preferably dry from head to toe.

From here on, the fun was limitless as we strapped on our ice-skates and began to explore the water ways, play ice hockey until we were blue in the face with the cold and generally tired and worn out from all the fun.

Another favourite of ours was to get on the ice planes which had come about when the fields were flooded as a form of providing nutrients for the grass and thus the cows during summer, which suited us nicely.

That is, apart from skating as far as the eye could see, we would also develop ice sails that could be used like any other sail to propel us along at speeds well in excess of 80 km per hour, back and forth and back again.

One day, it was just Gerhard, a younger mate of mine, and me on the ice plane, when we skated as far as we could, before we realized that it was getting dark and time to get back before walking home some 3 to 4 km.

There is one thing you may not know about the thickness of any ice, the development of which is subject to the flow of water, as in a creek that generally has thinner ice than its static counterpart or pond or lake.

And whilst we were fully aware of this, we were nevertheless witnessing a gradual decline in the light, which made it difficult for us to differentiate between the static water and the flowing canals and creeks.

And so we found ourselves in the middle of a canal when the ice gave away and we were up to our necks in the icy cold water, which didn't disturb us as we went through the routine of finding the nearest embankment.

In that context, it was simply a matter of trudging around in the belly deep mud so as to ascertain the direction of the incline before we would reach the edge of the canal and climb out of the mud, which also covered our clothes.

Frome here on, it was simply a matter of keeping warm, which we accomplished by skating back as fast as we could before we ran all the way home and announced ourselves to our parents, who couldn't be more delighted.

As it happened, our mud soaked clothes had frozen into a solid armour which had to be cut from our bodies before we would get a good belting, a wash and sent to bed, which was all in a days of hard fun on the ice.

If you are wondering how we kept warm in winter, the lounge room had a wood burner or coal burner with a flue that ran all the way to the ceiling and back again into the brick chimney, all of which gave off a lot of heat.

At the same time, the chimney was also collecting a lot of dust and grime that had to be removed once a year, usually in winter, by the chimney sweep who was wearing all black and no footwear of any kind.

The reason for this was basically for his safety when he climbed out of the attic onto the roof top and then towards the chimney, after which he applied one of his many tools of trade, hopefully without falling.

Other winter wonders may be associated with the falling snow, which may be beautiful when you are all snuggled in, but can be a pain in the arse when you have to ride your bicycle to school every weekday and back.

This was always the worst for the first bike in the morning which had to pave the way for the next, and so on, until there was a relatively good run of compacted snow for the remaining part of the day, which brings me to my father's VW.

You might remember me telling you about Hitler's secret weapon which was able to withstand any weather condition from the arctic to the deserts, that is, providing the cable brakes were not frozen into a solid mass.

Yet, there was one way to get the old beetle back on the road, and that was to pour hot water on the brakes from the pedal to the four wheels until they responded to the pedal action and the release of the hand brake.

As to our fun in response to the snow, we became hunters as we scrambled for our bows and arrows in readiness for the pursuit of hares, rabbits, pheasants and anything else that wasn't nailed down, like the odd pigeon.

In principle, we would follow the fresh track in the snow until they ended somewhere in a bush or a hole, and so we would surround the area before we made one hell of a racket in the hope that the poor animal might take off.

In reality, we never caught anything, which didn't really matter as we probably would not have been able to gut the animal before we took it home to our parents, who might have given us another good hiding in the bargain.

On Sundays, my brother and I would frequently go to the picture theatre where my father was a projectionist, and so we got in for free, which was great until my father got fired because he threatened to kill the boss.

Back to autumn and the time of year when the entire neighbourhood got into the spirit of marching around the streets with lanterns, singing songs like "Bumma la bumma Laterne, (Lantern) Sonne, (Sun) Mond (Moon) und Sterne. (Stars) That's all I know.

And whilst we left the singing to the conservatives, we would use the occasion to go round with smoke bombs made from tins that were open on one end and pierced with holes on the other so as to release the smoke from the smouldering wood inside.

This type of seasonal recreation was soon followed by St. Nicklaus day when we got dressed up in all sorts of fancy gear, the purpose of which was to be rewarded for our efforts by the neighbours whenever we knocked on their doors.

A favourite spot was the street in which the Americans had made their temporary homes, as they would normally invite us in to sing our little songs before we got rewarded with chocolate and lollies and other goodies.

At the end of the night, we would typically have a sack full of chocolate, sweets, biscuits and fruit that would last us for a long time to come, like a day or so.

Another cheerful event came along every year in the form of the "Freimarkt" or free market in October which was like the "Oktoberfest" in South Germany with the exception of the entertainment, most of which had to be paid for.

There were acres and acres of rides and sideshows that would always take us a number of days after school to explore, one of which was a sausage sizzle that was selling sausages made from horse meat – marvellous.

And then Christmas came along, when we put up a real Christmas tree from the forest with sweets hanging from the branches together with the usual crap that goes on Christmas trees, including 'real' candles.

That's right, real candles, which was dynamite when it came to the flammability of the tree, many of which caught fire, which was really funny until it happened in our house one year and all the presents got burnt.

In a good year, we would have to wait for Father Christmas to give us our presents on Christmas Eve, which was usually a neighbour who was well known to us whilst we had to put our little spiel across with words like:

"Dearest Father Christmas, don't look at me so angrily and please put your whipping stick away as I promise to be good the whole year round", at which we would cross our fingers behind our back in the true fashion of a non-believer.

And before you knew it, the end of the year had arrived with another type of entertainment in the form of firecrackers which we lit up before we placed them under a tin which was strategically positioned under a street light.

In doing so, the tin would go up like a rocket and hopefully hit the light which thankfully had been equipped with a guard around the globe so as to protect it from little shits like us.

On the whole, there was a lot of drinking and merriment all over the place, which led to many a headache the next morning, and I couldn't wait until I was old enough to join this annual ritual of madness and self-destruction.

At the same time, some of the destruction involved the odd thatch-roofed farmhouse, which didn't take too kindly to the odd firecracker landing on its roof, which led to a number of farmhouses burning down every year.

Other winter events consisted of company's arranging an annual 'Kohl & Pinkel Fahrt' (Cabbage & Haggis Walk) for their employees, whereby they got all dressed up as they marched through the suburbs to some pub.

Some of them had already started with the drinking as they passed through our street with noisy drums and rattle sticks whilst the Schnapps bottle was passed around; it makes you wonder how they got to where they were going.

I was still going to primary school, when my teacher discovered that I was writing left handed, which was 'verboten' at the time, and so I had to change my writing hand which led to my permanent crow's feet writing style.

The autocratic German style of running the country also made itself known in the Boy Scouts, of which my brother and I were a member, and we had many good experiences getting drenched on our way to some destination.

On one occasion, we had a general assembly when the boy next to me pinched my leg, which caused me to laugh; you would have thought World War 3 had broken out as the Commandant lost his cool.

And when I was stupid enough to owe up to the offending laugh, I was banned from attending the scouts for a month, whilst the bugger next to me got away Scott free; obviously, honesty doesn't pay.

By the time I was allowed back, spring had sprung and our group was heading off into some distant forest, where we built our tent and stripped naked as we ran around exploring the area, which I did together with a mate of mine.

Anyway, we got to this haystack which we decided to climb before we laid back in the hay, when all of a sudden my mate jumped on top of me and performed the weirdest ritual, as he thrust his erect penis onto my fragile body.

When he finally got off me, I thought that this must have been some kind of game that I had obviously missed out in my education, and so I left it with that.

Not long after that, my brother came home from the merchant navy and was telling me about all the different countries and places he had been, when he inquired about my association with the opposite sex.

Well, I hadn't as much as held the hand of a girl, not to mention the kissing, upon which he said he would show me how this was done as he placed his lips on mine and stuck his tongue down my throat –Yuck and triple Yuck.

I was not impressed as I swore to him I would never kiss a girl, if that is what all the fuss is about, and fair enough, it took me years before I even considered the thought.

My parents took my brother and me to the North Sea where they sat in a Sun Basket whilst we explored the sea shore and the mudflats which were exposed for kilometres all the way to some nearby islands.

In fact, they provided horse drawn carts for people to go to the islands, many of which would stay there overnight, whilst the water came back to the shore and thus cover the road through the mudflaps.

Apparently every year some fool or two ventured too far from the shore and got caught by the rising flood to the point where they either drowned or hung onto some post that had been erected for that very purpose.

Coming back to the money making schemes, we had a nine hole golf course nearby which we visited regularly to search for golf balls which we then sold back to the players at some strategic point on the course.

The main method was to get into the shallow ditches bordering the course, whereby there was a leader and three or four followers, meaning that the leader had the first pick by way of feeling the balls with his bare feet.

At the same time, we would keep an eye on the 'impact' side of the ditch, where the errand balls were often embedded in the embankment, whilst the leader was recycled every so often so as to give everyone an equal chance.

And then somebody had the bright idea to carve a club from the nearest tree so that one could bash into the ball, just like the real players were doing, that is, providing there was nobody on the course at the time.

This is when I rediscovered my left handedness as I held my superbly crafted club with a left-handed grip whilst I was using a right-handed swing, which somehow seemed to work for me after a bit of practice.

One of the players who was regularly buying balls from us suggested that we should go to the clubhouse and offer our services as 'Caddies', which was basically a matter of carrying the golf bags or pulling the golf buggies for the players.

This sounded like a good opportunity to me for making regular money, which I pursued to the point were I became a regular caddy every afternoon after school and every Saturday and Sunday, which I loved.

I even acquired a number of old golf clubs which I cherished and looked after with my life, whilst I was allowed to play golf myself and a couple of mates before the players started on Saturday and Sunday, where we caddied 18 holes. (2 times 9 holes)

We would then go out during lunch and play a few more holes in time to get back and caddy another 18 holes, after which we would resume play until it got dark and we staggered home exhausted but satisfied.

I eventually became the steady caddy for a gentleman by the name of Mr. Wilkens who was an old chap with a limp, which he received when he was playing hockey for Germany against Pakistan many years ago.

I was running late one Sunday morning when Mr. Wilkens turned up and was looking for me, upon which the caddy master informed him of my absence and the need to choose another caddy to replace me.

And with that, he pointed to one boy who flatly refused to take on the job, after which one after another boy refused in the same manner when I happened to come round the corner on my bike, which seemed to settle the matter.

As we walked to the first tee, Mr. Wilkens looked at me and said "What was that all about?" to which I replied that the other boys were stupid and he shouldn't take any notice of the matter, but he insisted on knowing the truth.

And so I reluctantly informed him that he was the lowest paying player in the club, which I personally didn't mind as I enjoyed his company and he was very kind to me, which was more important to me than money.

Nothing more was said on the subject until we finished our daily round and it was time for him to pay me, when he pressed a small number of notes into my hand, to which I replied that it was more than I was normally getting.

He insisted and paid me double from thereon, which really got up the noses of the other caddies, which was further exacerbated by the fact that he offered me to play golf with him on weekdays whenever he didn't have a partner.

I soon became a reasonable player, despite my unusual combination of left hander grip and right hander club, which eventually led to my being chosen for the annual caddy championship against the Hamburger caddies.

And whilst I didn't win the tournament, I managed to hit my ball in an awkward manner to the point where it hit my opponent and won me the game, despite the fact that I was well behind and in a hopeless position, such are the rules.

Strangely enough, the Bremer caddies, including me, were never officially taught anything about the rules, nor did the players instruct us when it came to the finer points of being a caddy, which really hit home one day.

That is, I was caddying for a lady who was playing in a club championship and one hole away from winning, when she was instructing me to go and hold the flag on the green whilst she was making her approach shot.

I did as I was told, when she hit the ball and it came racing towards the flag and I decided in my wisdom to take my hand off the flag stick in the knowledge that, if I had taken it out, the ball would have ended up over the green.

Little did I know that, once you have touched the flag pole, it must not be touched by a ball, in which case the lady's ball hit it square on and stopped close by, which made me really happy until I realized she had to forfeit the game.

And if you thought this type of incident would have caused the management to review their caddy training, or lack thereof, you are wrong, which is somewhat typical of that time when ignorance was the best policy, come what may.

I was in my last year at primary school when my parents decided to send me to a technical college to prepare me for a trade up to year ten, after which I would join the workforce in some kind of apprenticeship, which I didn't mind.

Anyway, my teacher wrote a letter to my parents suggesting that I should go on to high school as he would be able to get me a scholarship, which created bit of a stir in the family, as they thought they couldn't afford to support me.

And so they sat me down and explained the facts of life, upon which I assured them that I could support myself and they didn't have to fork out any money, as I was working on the golf course and doing other odd jobs.

OK then, if you are sure, they said, and so it was off to the best school in town, the Hermann Boese School, which was an all-boys school with an excellent reputation for shaping the minds of little smart-arses like me.

At the same time, I was fully aware of my government support status, which my main teacher 'Herr Schterzenbach' frequently reminded me of when I was not getting top marks in his favourite subject – Latin, which I hated.

He would look me straight in the eye and say crap like "Herr Strichow, you know and I know that you can do better, so please do, or I might have to inform the people that are paying for your fees", which really pissed me off.

And so I would apply myself for a while until I was back at the top of the class before I relapsed, and so the cycle kept on repeating itself, which was reflecting my attitude towards learning unless I really enjoyed the subject.

I didn't enjoy my German lesson on this one day when our teacher walked in with a handful of paintings which we had to write a "picture description" for as part of our test in German literature and writing of essays.

As it happened, we had never done this sort of picture description before, which left me more confused than most of my class mates who quickly took up the challenge with pages and pages of meaningless waffle.

As to my part, I was stumped as I was no good at waffling, nor was I any good at essays, which was reflected in my marks for the subject, yet I soon got the hang of it as I described this picture with geometrical accuracy.

That is, I measured all the key elements of the landscape in terms of their distance from the edge and each other, together with the colours, the description of each element and any other relevant information that came to mind.

And so the day of reckoning came, when I was told that I had failed the exercise in the worst possible manner, upon which I made an appointment with the school principle who somehow couldn't see my side of the story.

Needless to say, I hated my German teacher after that little incident, and I'm sure the feeling was mutual, as I received another lowest possible mark in my German class at the end of the year, which didn't surprise me.

I was better in my English class subject to the fact that I could roll the Rrrrrss like a mad-dog pirate, whilst I had to stand in front of the whole class and made to feel like the bloody idiot that I was at the time.

On the whole, I felt like a square peg in a round hole, as I was the only one in the class without a rich or famous parent, and whilst this didn't seem to bother me, it nevertheless gave me some kind of inferiority complex.

This was not helped by the fact that I was constantly surrounded by rich and famous people on the golf course, who had to invest a huge amount of money in the club before they were considered as fully-fledged members.

I guess, this accounts for my subsequent attitude towards life in general, and my desire to work hard and make something of myself, which is not to say that my main aim in life was to become rich and famous, like them.

On the contrary, I was quick to learn about the difference between lots of money and lots of happiness, the latter of which is associated with 'Our Ultimate Purpose in Life' and the pursuit of a common goal.

In that context, many of the rich and famous were missing the point of living altogether as they focused single-mindedly on the accumulation of wealth, if need be at the expense of others, which makes for a miserable existence.

Back to my school, we used to go to yearly camps which, on one occasion, was cursed from start to finish as we found out when we stopped on a canal bridge to observe a barge that was about to go under the bridge.

And just when the barge was right below us, this stupid idiot decided to release his spit, which landed right in the eye of the skipper, who was not too pleased as he shouted his disgust with the youths of the day.

Well, this hurt the pride of our 'Herr Schterzenbach' who informed us in no uncertain terms that the trip was cancelled unless the perpetrator came forward there and then, which he did with words like "It could have been me".

And so we continued with our ill-fated trip until we arrived to this lake where we had been booked into a lodge that was to be our home for the next few days, and you will never guess what came next.

That is, we all ran around like mad dogs when we came across this war time ammunition dump, which delighted us no end as we dug up the phosphor bombs and other bombs from their hiding of some 10 years or more.

We then distributed the bombs amongst ourselves as we proceeded to hide behind trees and throw the bombs at each other, which was one hell of a stupid thing to do, and I still don't know how we managed to survive.

Just as well, Herr Schterzenbach came over the hill and saw what was going on and stopped us instantly, or I might not be telling you the story of my funny little life, unless you were in hell, as I would have been for sure.

Needless to say, we were told the riot act and punished for our stupidity, beginning with the cancellation of our school trip and a bloody good hiding from our parents when we arrived early back home and the truth got out.

As to Herr Schterzenbach, he demanded that we read the papers for the next month and cut out all the ammunition related injuries and deaths, of which there was a staggering amount all over the countryside, which blew us away.

By all accounts, there was a huge amount of ammunition, bombs and Booby-traps like fountain pens that had been dropped by enemy planes, which were meant to explode in your face once you removed the cover.

Much of that was found on the railway lines where the troops had just thrown their unwanted gear out the window, which created a kind of 'After-war' effect, much of which was felt by innocent or ignorant children like us.

On a happier note, I was earning enough money to buy myself a second hand 50 cc motorbike or Moped, as they were called, which didn't have to be registered, nor did you have to have a licence or pay any fees.

Apart from exploring the area, I used the Moped to take my yearly holiday trip to the Alps involving some 2,000 km return trip which I had undertaken in the previous year on a bicycle, where we had to do 100 km per day minimum.

We would stay in youth hostels and live on jam sandwiches with the odd splurge on the local foods like the Vienna Schnitzel in one town that was renowned for it, whilst drinking the odd Stein or litre of the local beer, or two or more.

I remember on our last Moped trip, we came to a town called 'Ruedesheim' right on wine festival time, which we took on with a vengeance that I shall never forget, like the night when I drank three bottles of the newly brewed wine.

The circumstances were such that my mates took to the local girls as they danced and wore off the effects of the wine, whilst I was sitting at the table and enjoying the local drop, which was nice and mellow, not unlike a fruit drink.

From hereon, everything went a little hazy for the next three days as I had never drunk any wine before and was now suffering from alcohol poisoning that reminded me of the time when I had eaten Nightshade berries.

For three days I lay next to this rubbish bin lifting my head every so often so as to make my miserable deposits, which I didn't know where they were coming from, as I was obviously depleted and unable to give anymore.

It took me some time before I touched that stuff again, which might have saved me a lot of money, as many a wine drinker will tell you as he lies on the side of the street and begs you to give him some money to support his habit.

I was now 18 years old and ready to make my mark with the opposite sex as my mate and I strolled into the local brothel which consisted of a bombed out dead end street where 'the girls' were displaying their wares in the cellars.

There seemed to be a particularly good girl at the end of the street, as there was a queue in front of this particular cellar, and we soon discovered the reason when a gorgeous blonde invited the next bloke into her room.

We noticed an old gentleman who was at the end of the line with a walking stick, without which he would have surely fallen over, hopefully for the last time on top of a beautiful blonde, after which he would have been happy to die.

And whilst it took him a long time to get to the front, his dream was ultimately shattered by the busty blond, as she refused to take him on, regardless of his pleading and willingness to pay whatever it took, but to no avail.

As for me, I didn't have enough money to afford such quality, and so we went to the other end where the prices were cheaper, when I discovered this voluptuous female with a bosom that was spilling out over the top of her dress.

Luckily, the price was right, and so my mate wished me well as I was about to make my debut as a lover, which I proceeded to do as I entered her little den and paid her the money in anticipation of what lay ahead.

And with that, she took off her dress and her 'Buestenhalter', (bras) when I discovered her disfigurement as her breasts hit the floor, after which I ran for my life back up the stairs, without asking for a refund or replacement.

Needless to say, that took the wind out of my sails for a while until my two best mates and I decided to rent a car and take a trip to the red light district in Hamburg, where the 'real prostitutes' were hanging out, literally.

Anyway, we began our night of pleasure by getting into one of these girly bars, where you bought girls expensive drinks which we later discovered to be cold tea, whilst we built up our courage with a 'Schnapps' or two.

It wasn't long until my mate inquired about the bill, which had reached astronomic heights without us having had as much as kissed a girl, never mind touching them in some way, and so we paid our dues and left in a hurry.

Having had a few drinks, we thought we would go straight to where the action was, namely in the 'Herbertstrasse' which was barred for anybody below 18, as it clearly stated on the gates at either end of the street.

As far as my sexual expertise was concerned, I had made some inquires with the studs in my neighbourhood who were giving me conflicting information about the art of lovemaking, which I was about to regret.

That is, considering I was an "Independent-minded person, a thinker and a doer with little time for the established ways of doing things, unless they are personally tried and proven", I proceeded to make a fool of myself once again.

We walked up and down a few times before one of my mates made his choice in the form of a busty beauty which he consumed in an apparent ten minutes of passion, after which he reappeared with a huge grin on his face.

One down, two to go, which was myself and a catholic boy who had an internal struggle with God who wouldn't allow him to become a man, which was something I never suffered from, as I chose the target for my affections.

After negotiating the price, I entered her little boudoir where she sat on her couch waiting for me to make the first move, which was not in my instruction manual, and so I sat there talking about life and shit like that.

After a minute or so she said something like "Are you here to shag me or not?" which didn't do much for my confidence as I undressed with my back to her, whilst she dropped her flimsy gown and lay back on the couch.

What comes next is embarrassing for the male population as I proceeded to mount her in a variety of positions that were not even mentioned in the Kama Sutra, upon which she asked if I actually knew what I was doing.

Well, that together with my slow start and the alcohol that was making itself known in the downstairs area was enough for me to withdraw from the scene, as I thanked her for her time and proceeded to leave.

In doing so, I ruffled my hair, slapped my face a couple of times so as to obtain a state of exhaustion before I staggered out the door with a satisfied (artificial) grin on my face, which was duly applauded by my two mates.

As to my catholic mate, God won the battle that night, which he regretted all the way home that night back to Bremen, and we were sick and tired of hearing about his "I could have shagged them all, but I didn't want to".

We all could have killed him that night, but we didn't want to, as our God would have never forgiven us, whatever we perceived him, her or them to be.

My father's film business had gone broke soon after that, and there was a feud developing between my father and his mate with the aunt in America, who had put up the money for the venture, and so things weren't good.

It seemed like nobody really got on with my father from his mate to our neighbours, relatives and anybody else with a bit of common decency in his mind, which prompted my father to apply for an apartment in a high-rise building.

In the meantime, my brother had emigrated to Australia on a two year assisted passage, and he was telling us in glowing terms about his life in Melbourne which, if half of it was true, was still one hell of a place to be living.

He told us he was living in a large house, had two cars and played tennis most of the time, whilst enjoying the sunshine, going to the beach and generally living a life that was beyond our wildest imagination.

And so the decision was made for the family to join him as soon as possible and to apply for an assisted passage with the Australian department of immigration, whilst I was to stop my education and find a job to get some money.

As it happened, I was in year twelve and not far from matriculation, but this was not an issue as the family came first and I personally didn't care, as I was looking forward to the adventure and the chance for a new life.

I applied for a number of jobs, one of which was with a large import company which was owned by a family for which I was occasionally caddying on the golf course, however, they obviously did not know of my application.

There was a room full of well dressed gentlemen, when I burst in with my mate on the way home from an indoor swimming pool with wet hair, ruffled street clothing and a towel under my arm, and I thought I had come to the wrong place.

And whilst I was actually in the right place and left my details and lack of experience with the man during a brief interview, he seemed to like the fact that I had been at the Hermann Boese School, which was always highly regarded.

At the same time, I didn't get any response which led to my getting a job with a coffee and chocolate wholesaler, where I got my first taste of the real world, which I enjoyed immensely due to the warmth of the people.

My job was varied as I was strapping boxes one day, replenishing stocks another day and generally became a dogsbody who was doing everything and anything, which was really satisfying as I got along well with everybody.

I was working with a boy who had lost his father in the war, and he hadn't come to terms with it as he frequently showed signs of his social disorientation like when I caught him throwing knifes at the coffee boxes in the store room.

He seemed to be crying out for help, and we found out more about his lonely life with his mother after a beer or two in the local pub, which we frequented every Friday night after work where we hung out until we had skin full.

On this particular Friday night, I had been overdoing it a little too much as I staggered down the road towards the nearest bus stop, when this car pulled up and Herr Schterzenbach opened the door and offered me a lift.

Well, what can I say other than that I was going through the floor as it appeared as though the government had wasted its money on me, as Herr Schterzenbach proceeded to tell me in no uncertain terms, and I was too drunk to argue the point.

Back to my job, it was time for the Christmas season and the preparation of orders which we were doing flat out, when I was working in the packing room with a mate and suggested we practice the little 'English' we knew.

And so the swearing went back and forth as we went about our work, whilst we raised our voices as an expression of our enthusiasm for the English language, when the big boss walked in and demanded what in the hell was going on.

We duly informed him of our English speaking attempt, which calmed him down as he gave us some advice with respect to our responsibility towards other people and the company as he left, when I observed a smile on his face.

He was an excellent boss and we all revered him for his fairness and ability to get the best out of his people, regardless of the pressure they might have been under at the time, which is something I rarely experienced in later life.

Also, the camaraderie of the people I worked with was exceptional, which became obvious when we were accepted by the Australian Government and I had to give notice in mid December 1999, as we had to get ready to leave.

And then I got this letter to tell me that I had been successful with my job application with this large import company, which I had forgotten about and was now informing of my inability to go through with it.

I was selling all my possessions like my bike, Moped and whatever I had of any value, after which I gave the money to my father so that he could pay for the trip, which all worked out pretty well as we approached the departure date.

As far as my friends and relatives were concerned, we were all mad to leave the 'Vaterland', which was also sneered upon by the conservative element of the community, not to mention the ruination of my brilliant career.

I was surprised to find out that my mates at the wholesaler had arranged a going away party at the local watering hole which was presenting a Bavarian style of food and drinking environment which was always very jolly.

And then my workmates came along one by one as they presented me with a token of their friendship in the form a gift that was typical of the Bremen culture and tradition, which I will never forget as long as I life.

At the end of the evening, I was informed that 'the night had just begun', as they ushered me into a car and took me to a dance hall, where there was and additional crowd of people from my place of work, which really threw me.

And to top it off, they informed me that this particular girl seemed to have a crush on me and she was ready to go all the way as a going away present which I would never forget, if only I had the guts to go through with it.

That is, in the light of my last encounter with the opposite sex, I was ready to join the priesthood, as I was obviously not meant for any kind of fatherhood or sexual intercourse, as I had proven on several occasions.

Not to worry, I had a wonderful evening as I was told the next morning when I woke up next to one of the boys from work, who had kindly agreed to put me up in his bed, considering I was out to it for the latter part of the night.

As to the people in the neighbourhood, I don't think they were all that sorry to see us go, apart from my best mate Klaus who offered to drive us all the way to Bremerhaven near the North Sea, where the ship was anchored.

At that moment, we discovered that the ship by the name of 'Castle Felice' had been deployed previously to take my brother to America, where he had jumped ship to explore the country, until he got caught at the Mexican Border.

He was consequently deported on the very same ship back to Germany where he went back to sea, whilst my step sister was on the next trip to America in order to take up a childcare position with the German Ambassador.

When her contract was finished, she returned to Germany on the same Castle Felice, where she renewed many of her acquaintances with the crew, which hadn't changed much then, which also applied to our journey.

Given my half sister was now going to Australia, there was a new sense of reunion as we set off for the adventure of a lifetime, beginning with our passage through the Bay of Biscay, which was renowned for its stormy weather.

This became obvious as the old ship was trying to stay afloat that night whilst we lay in our beds and felt the swaying of the ship from side to side with a creaking and groaning that seemed to signal the end of our little lives.

And every time we thought the final moment had come, the old ship somehow managed to right itself before it went to the other side, and so the night went on as we rushed to the toilet every so often to spew our guts out.

Well, we survived that part of our journey as we passed the Rock of Gibraltar on our way through the Mediterranean Sea to the Suez Canal, where we stopped in Addis-Ababa, the capital of Ethiopia, and went on shore.

This was quite a new world for me as the local traders swarmed upon us with a variety of goods and services which we had never seen or experienced before, one of which was a little boy who offered me some Spanish Fly.

I had learned about this aphrodisiac in my dealings with the local experts who assured me that this was a sure way to get a girl into bed, which I still had a problem with, as you are well aware of, and so I decided to buy one.

As it turned out later, I had bought a Vitamin pill that had no effect on the female population unless it was wrapped up in a $100 note, and so I resigned myself once again to the fact that I was definitely not going to be a real man.

We passed safely through the Suez Canal as we watched the camels and Palm trees go by, all of which was wrapped in a desert of sand that went on and on all the way to the Red Sea on our way to the Indian Ocean.

And whilst we had been enjoying the ship's food and diet consisting of meat, potatoes and frozen vegetables, we would have given our right arm for something fresh, like an apple, a peach or similar change of diet.

At least we didn't suffer from any scurvy like our forefathers on their voyage to Australia, as we were given plenty of lemons to suck on, which helped to wipe the smile off our faces as we broke down in the middle of the Indian Ocean.

We floated helplessly for a couple of days as the crew tried to repair the clapped out engine for the third time on this journey alone, which left us to wonder whether we would ever make it to the promised land called Australia.

Luckily, the engine was repaired (barely) as we struggled along on half power when we eventually arrived in Freemantle, where we experienced the Australian hospitality for the first time, together with the brilliant sunshine.

I remember walking into G J Coles to buy some sweets, which was not something I had ever experienced on that scale, nor did I expect the easygoing way of the Aussies who seemed to have a bottomless pit of friendliness.

We were chosen as a family of typical migrants and had our picture published in the local paper, which was exciting as we continued our journey through the Australian Bait towards Melbourne, our final destination.

And then we arrived on the 26th of January 1960, where it was a public holiday or Australia Day and I saw my brother on dry land as we approached the Station Pier on this fantastic summer day, which I shall never forget.

Nor will I ever forget the first words my brother said to me through the open porthole as he was inquiring about my financial status, to which I replied that I had saved the incredible amount of three pounds Australian currency.

With that, I handed over my precious savings as my brother explained that this might be enough for the petrol to get us to the opposite end of town to a suburb called Regent, where we were going to stay for a while.

We were all absorbed by the novelty of it all, when we had to stop in Clifton Hill at a red light and this bloke walked up to my brother and threatened to kill him if he didn't receive his money before the week was out.

Fortunately, my parents didn't understand the gist of the conversation, and so the episode was swept under the carpet for the time being as we proceeded towards our destination, as in the big house in which my brother lived.

And again, the reality hit home as we were welcomed by Mrs. Gross and her husband who had emigrated from Latvia some 10 years ago and were now running a boarding house for migrants like us, which came as a bit of a shock.

To be specific, the boarders (all male) were stacked into small rooms four at a time, which left the lounge room for us to call home for a week or so whilst we slept on the floor and my father was looking for a place to rent.

As to the two cars which my brother owned, the second car was for the spare parts which seemed to fall off his main car with monotonous regularity and it had to be towed back from wherever he happened to break down.

His passion with the tennis game also unfolded into a big fat lie before long as he couldn't tell one end of the racket from another, nor could he afford the cost of playing the game, as he was barely able to pay for his living.

It didn't take long for my father to find a suitable house in Reservoir, where we moved soon after together with couple of boarders who had been on the ship with us, and my brother who wasn't ready to move back with my father.

And so it didn't take long before my brother told me of his plan to go to Queensland, where you could make lots of money cutting sugar cane together with his mate Horst, who he had known for some time already.

His plan was to roll the car out of the driveway backwards onto the main road without starting the motor, the purpose of which was not to awaken my father, whilst I was giving him a push from the front, which went off without a hitch.

In the morning, my father discovered the missing son and car as he put two and two together before he asked me whether I had any idea of the plan, to which I assured him that I was as shocked as he was about the fact that my brother had escaped once again.

Two days later in the evening, there was a knock on the door from the Clifton Hill bloke who threatened to kill my brother unless . . . . ,upon which my father informed him that the bird had flown, which the guy refused to believe.

"We have you surrounded, so don't give me no shit!" he said as he pointed to his cronies who were hanging around the place, and so my father invited them into house, sat them down and proceeded to inquire about their grievances.

They eventually calmed down as they commiserated with my father over a beer or two, and so they left without tearing the house apart, for which I admired my father with respect to his cool handling of the situation.

My first job was not far away with a company called Brownbuilt who was manufacturing filing cabinets and my job was to assist the press operator with the stacking of his panels and work in progress, which was hard work for me.

After all, I had never worked 8 hours without a break other than a short tea break and half hour lunch, but I soon got the hang of it whilst I considered my future, which was obviously not in my present capacity as a labourer.

As I was now earning a regular income, I was able to buy a second hand motor scooter, which I drove around the neighbourhood until I felt confident enough to go for my license in the city, where I failed my written test.

And so I brushed up on the rules in readiness for my next appointment, where I passed the written test, upon which the big burly policeman told me to go outside and start my bike, which became a bit disaster in its own right.

That is, my bike had broken down the day before, which had led to my taking the train to town in the naïve state of mind that the test people would supply the necessary vehicle or other mode of transport, including a scooter.

And as I couldn't find a scooter of any kind outside, I thought that he must have meant the police bike, which I tried to start by jumping on the starter pedal. (without a key or any knowledge of how to drive the damn thing)

What I also didn't realize is the fact that I was not allowed to take on a pillion passenger in the first year, as I assumed in my innocence that the big burly policeman would be sitting behind me and direct me through the course.

This is when the policeman came out and found me jumping up and down on his bike, to which he inquired about 'my' bike, and so I told him that my scooter had broken down, but that should not affect my driving test.

With that, he went back into the office where I heard a thunder of laughter, and for a minute I had no idea what they might be laughing about, but I was soon made aware of my mistake as he told me to come back when the bike was fixed.

The next week, I was back with my bike and I finally got my license, which allowed me to look further afield for work, which soon led to my getting a job in Port Melbourne with a sandwich machine company.

The idea was to make the machine and place it into strategic areas like canteens and airports etc., upon which the machine was filled daily with fresh sandwiches in a cardboard container, which was a great idea – on paper.

I met a German fellow there by the name of Helmut who was soon to become my best mate, as we saw each other after work, where I found out about his passion for the classic guitar, which he wanted to involve me with.

And so I rehearsed together with him on the guitar and me on the Bongos, which I could barely play as we tried to sing in harmony all sorts of music from a Spanish selection, of which he had many records and music sheets.

One day he announced that we were booked at the Colping House, which was a German run boarding house that had a dance evening once every month, which made me rather nervous, as I had no faith in my musical skills.

Well, the evening might have been a success for Helmut, but it was disaster for me as I sat there with my Bongos on my knees and proceeded to make a fool of myself, once again, whilst everybody seemed to feel sorry for me.

So much for my brilliant musical career, which was soon followed by the collapse of the sandwich machine company due to the simple fact that they could not get the mechanism to work, and so I was looking for a job once again.

And to make matters worse, my scooter had also broken down, which was entirely my fault as I was not familiar with a two stroke engine and the need to keep an eye on the motor oil in the sump and to replenish any losses.

This had never been a requirement or problem with my Moped in Germany, which was equipped with a four-stroke engine, where the oil was mixed in with the petrol, and so there was no need to top up any sump oil.

The problem became obvious when the motor ceased up one day because the piston overheated and got stuck in the cylinder head, which seemed to heal itself after a few minutes when I tried to restart the engine.

And so I went on with my stop-start Hoppidihop approach of returning home and to the nearest garage until the conrod connecting the piston with the crankshaft broke, and I had to call upon a mate to tow me home.

To make matters worse, I could not get any spare parts here in Australia or even overseas, which left me with the only choice under the circumstances in the form of welding the conrod, which was not a reliable process.

Anyway, this got me back on the road as I was now applying for a job with the National Cash Register Company as a technician, which I was successful in after some rigorous testing of my analytical skills, which I passed with flying colours.

I was now working at head office in Russell Street where I learned the ropes whilst I was going to specific training courses beginning with the repair and maintenance of the simplest models, followed by the next, and so on.

It didn't take me long to become proficient to the point were I was sent to Warragul in the Gippsland Ranges where I was staying in the Railway Hotel and helping the local representative with his territorial tasks.

I have failed to mention the beginning of my love affair with the girl next door in Reservoir, who was later to become my wife and mother of my children, after a courtship that lasted some five years when we got married in 1965.

Anyway, I was getting on my scooter every Friday night to be with my girl over the weekend, after which I returned to Warragul on Sunday night, which went on for a number of months until I was recalled to head office.

Under the circumstances, I was back living with my parents who had moved to Caulfield near the racecourse at a time when my brother had joined the Australian Navy and I had no more need for my scooter, and so I sold it.

The main reason for this was associated with the welded conrod or connecting rod which could break any moment, after which I would have had to throw the damn thing on the rubbish tip, as there was no other option.

It was then that my brother turned up in his Royal Australian Navy uniform, which seemed to impress the girls no end wherever we went, whilst I sat back and admired his ability to impress the opposite sex.

I had just settled in when the people upstairs asked my brother and me to join them at the beach together with the girl that lived upstairs who I had not yet met, and her cousin from Broken Hill who was there over the holidays.

We accepted, and so it was off to the beach, where we got to know the girls better and seemed to be getting along quite well before it was time to go home on this hot summer day, which was followed by a sultry night.

Under the circumstances, my brother and I decided to go to the local shop and buy some refreshments, when we noticed the girls sitting on the balcony wanting to know what we were up to and where we were going.

When we told them, they asked us to bring them back a Coke, which we did in due course as we delivered the goods by climbing the stairs to the balcony, when the girl living upstairs gave me the biggest kiss.

Well, that unsettled me somewhat as my brother and I lay in the backyard, which was separated from the upstairs people by a six foot fence, that is, until it got dark and we tried to get some sleep in the open air.

It was then that my brother tapped me on the arm and told me of his plan, which involved 'me' climbing the fence to see whether the girls were also sleeping in the yard, in which case there might have been further action.

As I was a fool by nature and always willing to fire somebody else's bullet, I proceeded to jump the fence to inspect the people sleeping on the ground, when I found out that the girls were not amongst them.

Not happy with that, my brother urged me to climb the stairs to the front balcony, where I found the two girls soundly asleep, which gave me the brilliant idea to kiss the upstairs girl in the neck in the full knowledge that she would be pleased.

Considering the two girls looked very much alight during the day, and especially in the moonlight, I had accidently kissed the cousin from Broken Hill who somehow did not appreciate the mix-up as she yelled out for her mother.

I quickly retreated and reported back to my brother who suggested that we might leave it with that and see what the next day brought, which we did as I was having visions of a disaster in the making, which didn't help with my sleep.

When I came home the next day, my father unceremoniously greeted me at the door with the biggest belting I had ever received, whilst he informed me of the fact that the upstairs girl's father was going to kill me, which didn't seem to bother him.

As I was frequently doing a bit of running around the racecourse, I decided to do so this evening so as to delay my imminent death, when I saw the whole family on the balcony waiting for my return and their revenge.

And every time I got past my place, they were there steadfast ready for me, and so I continued with my round until it eventually got dark and there were no more people on the balcony, and so I returned home.

As my brother had returned to his naval base and ship that day, I could not consult him with respect to my situation as I lay there in bed wondering what to do with myself, when suddenly I had this brilliant idea.

That is, I thought to myself "What what my brother do under the circumstances?" and then it came to me in a flash – he would pack his things and run for his life, which is exactly what I did as I jumped out the window with my suitcase.

I then hitchhiked to the other side of town at 2 o'clock in the morning where I slept in a park until it was a reasonable time to front up at my recently married step sister's house in Bundoora where she lived with her husband.

And that is where I stayed whilst the dust was settling in Caulfield, which eventually led to my visiting my parents who were happy to see me, whilst I made it quite clear that I was happy where I was now.

Soon after that, I bought myself a second hand Skoda, which I picked up in Melbourne without having a vehicle licence or as much as driven a car, but that didn't seem to bother the salesman, nor did it bother me.

I Kangaroo-hopped all the way back to Bundoora, where I began to learn how to drive a car, all on my own – of course, as if there was any other way.

My sister Rosi was married to a German called Wolly who was mad on hunting, and my brother and I were invited to join him and his mate Wombat shooting, which we did in my new second hand Skoda where the front window could be opened.

And so we went off this night to a spot where the Wombats were known to hang out, as Wolly headed off in one direction and we in another, after which we were supposed to meet up again at the very same spot.

And then we came across this poor creature that looked like a stuffed wombat as it sat on the side of the road as innocent as lamb, and I shot him dead as my brother had urged me to do, which was a really stupid thing to do.

Well, we loaded the body into the booth of the car where it proceeded to bleed like a pig, whilst we returned to the meeting place where Wolly and his mate finally turned up empty handed, and so they congratulated us.

Back home, we pulled the dead wombat from the bloodied booth and put it on the ground as we staggered to our beds, where I had all sorts of weird dreams about killing and being killed.

In the morning, the Wombat had swollen to twice its size, and when I asked Wolly what I was to do with it now, he simply told me that I was the hunter and I should have thought of that before I killed it—bloody hell.

I then disposed of the body in a nearby tip before trying to remove all the blood from the booth, which was virtually impossible as it had leaked into all the nooks and crannies, where it stayed as the car stank for the next six months.

That was the last time I ever killed anything, not that I never felt like killing some of the nasty people I met later in my life, as you will find out later on when I tell you about some of the strange people I ended up working for.

This reminds me of the night my mother rang me up crying as she pleaded for my help because dad was threatening to kill her and my little sister, who had fled to the neighbour where they were save for the moment.

Instead of ringing the police, I rushed over in my car where I found the house in total darkness, when I then opened to the front door which led straight into the sitting room where I saw the outline of my father in a chair.

As I walked across to him, I asked him whether he was alright, to which he mumbled that he was and why I was asking such a stupid question for, and so I told him that Mum had rung me and informed me otherwise.

Not knowing what to do, I left and waited in the car to see what was going to happen next, when the light went on and my father erupted into one of his extreme tempers before my mother and sister came running out of the house.

They headed straight for the neighbour and I was about to go after them when my father left the house and reversed his car out of the driveway, where he was about to spot me, and so I left the scene in a hurry.

Apparently, things settled down soon after as they had a hundred times before, which nevertheless needed the replacement of most of the sitting room furniture that could be lifted and thrown around the room.

I had known Marion (the girl next door) by then for 2 to 3 years, during which we had a lot of fun riding around on the scooter, which we now pursued further and further into the country side, where we often slept in the car overnight.

This didn't seem to worry her mother who had seven kids in total, the eldest of which, a boy, was living with a religious group in the country, whilst she was a widow who was struggling to make ends meet.

Part 2

LIFE IS ALL ABOUT "FRUSTRATION"

It was round about then that I could see myself settling down and building a house, as I bought a block of land in Greensborough which I paid off in a couple of years, whilst Marion and I got engaged.

I had also begun to take private lessons in mechanical engineering and drafting with the intentions of getting out of the lacklustre technician position with NCR and into a higher paying position as a budding engineer.

The advantage of being with a private tutor was that he could gauge the advancing skills of his pupils, which he could then recommend to whoever was looking for such skills, which led to my getting a job as a junior draftsman.

As I was quick on the uptake and going to night school at RMIT in town, I was soon adding to my responsibilities, for which I then approached the big boss who reluctantly offered me one pound at a time.

At the same time, he boasted that, if his last boss had not refused him his last request for a raise, he would still be working for that company, which didn't quite fit in with my perception of 'Fair pay for Fair work'.

I was also doing some part time drafting work at the time, which gave me the chance to pay for the block of land and gauge my value as a budding engineer who nevertheless didn't have a certificate or a diploma.

I got married in 1965 and built a house on my block in Greensborough together with my wife Marion, when I was starting to develop a sense of responsibility relating to paying a mortgage and the possibility of raising a family.

And then my part time boss offered me a job with his consulting business, which I accepted despite the promises of my boss, who was intimating that I would be running his business one day, even though he had a son.

Somehow, I had a problem with his concept of having to prove my value to the company and then get a raise 'One Pound at a Time' regardless of my true value, which was against my principles and started to frustrate me.

As to my job with the consulting business, the activities were entirely associated with the domestic natural gas conversion in the late 1960s, which went on until it came to a halt altogether at around the 1970s.

As my work involved the subcontracting of a variety of secondary operations, including drilling holes in cast iron burner heads and a variety of gas injectors, I could see an opportunity to earn some extra money.

This is when I discovered my calling in life or person who is *"Independent-minded, a thinker and a doer with little time for the established ways of doing things',* as you are about to find out in my endeavours to make money.

To be specific, I developed a number of 'ingenious' devices that allowed me to do some of these operations at home without having to invest any more than a few dollars, which I quickly recovered over the first batch.

I even built a machine from timber, steel and four second hand washing machine motors that were fitted out with a drill chuck and was operated by a lever to drill four holes at a time whilst the burner head was retained in a drill jig.

Prior to this, my boss informed me of an old 'Business Card Printing Machine' which was no longer working and getting in the way, and so he offered it to me as scrap and potential bits and pieces for my little home made contraptions.

And whilst I didn't have any use for the machine at the time, I took it home and pulled it to pieces, considering it was for free, and there was no further call for this type of machine, as it was well out date and no longer viable.

I was making good money at home, which soon came to the attention of my boss who turned out to be a nasty piece of work as I was gradually coming to realize, beginning with his claim that the drilling machine was actually 'his'.

To be specific, he was under the misguided impression that I had built the drilling machine from the bits and pieces of his 'Business Card Printer' which he had so generously 'lent' me, and was now insisting on getting back.

I was flabbergasted as I piled all the bits and pieces on a trailer and proceeded to take them to the factory he had hired by then, where I dumped them right in the middle of the loading bay and informed him of their return.

Well, he hadn't planned for that, which nevertheless left a bad taste in my mouth as I was now aware of the fact that I was working for a devious bastard who was out to screw people in a way that would make the devil proud.

As expected, the natural gas conversion eventually came to a close, upon which he informed me with respect to our need to reinvent the business in some other area of expertise in the hope that I might have some ideas on the matter.

All I knew was about the niche business opportunity relating to my previous place of employment, where I had been instrumental in the product design aspect and the general costing of the manufacturing processes.

He asked me "How much venture capital do you need to break into this market?" and so I told him my estimate based on the purchasing of the components making up the final product, whilst we were doing the assembly.

Done, he said, go and start selling yourself to the contacts that you know of, and the designs which you see fitting into our mode of manufacture, which I did post hast before coming back with a number of sizeable orders.

Under the circumstances, I concentrated my selling efforts in the Sydney area because we didn't want the customers to know of our micro-start in a business that needed substantial expertise and manufacturing facilities.

The venture started to take off as we rented a larger factory for the product assembly and light machining operations, where I concentrated on the sales and marketing side as well as the product design, subcontracting and production.

I was constantly intrigued by the sheer audacity of the boss, as you can see when I had an inquiry for 1,000,000 products by one company, who had also requested a minimum of four samples before they considered our quote.

And when the samples were completed, he sent me to the potential customer with a delivery docket stating that the samples had to be returned as delivered, that is, without having been tested other than in a visual fashion.

The boss thought that this was a stroke of genius as he was fully aware of the purpose of the samples, which was essentially to test them to the point of destruction, after which they could not be 'returned as delivered'.

Hence, the company would have been forced to give us the order, well, that is what he thought, which turned out to be another one of his stupid mistakes reflecting his evil intents and desire to exploit other people.

This brings me to my own stupidity and pride in my work, as I committed myself with a twelve hour week day and every weekend, during which my wife and newly born child joined me at the factory to help out – for free.

Apart from that, I was also using 'my' car and petrol for the purpose of delivering and picking up goods, which didn't seem to be appreciated until I complained about the petrol cost and he offered to reimburse me for that.

At the same time, he was telling me of this club to which he supposedly went every Friday night as a cover for his encounter with a high profile prostitute who was paid in the form of an undisclosed cheque in an envelope.

And if the amount was not in the top ten clients, you would not be allowed back; so much for the oldest profession in the world and the principle of 'supply and demand', or model of price determination in a free market economy.

This was a far cry from the raise of 'one pound at a time' scenario, providing you had proven your worth, which I had been exposed to in the past as I was now ready to change as a guiding principle in life.

And then the car broke down subject to the heavy duty application for which it was not designed, upon which I informed the boss and he commiserated without offering any kind of replacement, which really pissed me off.

And so I made him aware of the fact that our little venture was coming to an end unless he spent some money on a second hand VW kombi, to which he reluctantly agreed and generously allowed me to take it home.

Soon after that he called me into his office and made me an offer that, according to him, I couldn't possibly refuse, as he was about to show me his gratitude for all my hard work and the fact that I had created his new business.

With that, he informed me that his accountant had told him he was making too much money and the fact that he should engage in some kind of tax dodge which involved the purchase of a Laundromat that was making a $6,000 loss.

He then informed me of his generous offer in the form of my 10% ownership of the ill fated Laundromat, whilst he was nevertheless relieving me of the 10% of the losses for which he was more than willing to pay.

Well, that night my wife and I had a good old laugh as we contemplated my brilliant career with 'The Arsehole from Hell', which was becoming more and more obvious as I continued to work for him like the idiot that I was.

We were still living in Greensborough at the time when my wife had the bright idea to move to the Dandenong Ranges, where we built a new house in a tranquil dead end street, where we lived for the next 35 years or so.

The land was basically overrun with blackberries and covered with debris from a condemned house that had been demolished some time ago without clearing the half acre block, which was now our first port of call and task.

In view of our last owner-building in Greensborough and the knowledge gained from that, we were now better equipped to deal with the challenges associated with the preparation of the block and the need to plan well ahead.

In doing so, I proceeded to make a scaled model of the block, which I then 'graded' by shaping the model clay to where it might have been wanted in order to make place for the house and the drive way and carport, etc.

I then made a scaled model of our dream house, together with mini furniture, a fireplace, kitchen, laundry and the rest, whilst being mindful of our little budget, which unfortunately didn't include the double gabled roof.

When the boss's wife inquired about our progress, I informed her of the roof, upon which she talked to her husband to the point where they offered to pay for the roof, considering we were all helping out in the business—for free.

And then we had to take one Sunday off so that we could talk to the builder, considering I was working in the factory every night and with the family every week end, which left us with no time to do this type of building discussion.

Well, you should have seen the boss and his stupid wife on Monday morning as they greeted me at the door with words like "Where were 'You' yesterday when we needed you at the factory?" which really floored me.

When I told them of my need to meet up with the builder, his wife became hysterical whilst she informed me in no uncertain terms "If that is the way you are repaying us for taking care of the roof, you can just forget about it!"

Now, there is only so much you can kick a horse before it bolts, which is exactly what I did there and then as I informed the pair that I was leaving, without notice, and not to expect me back – ever, which is exactly what I did.

It might not have been the smartest way of dealing with the situation, but I just had enough of the pair of them, which nevertheless left me without a job and an income, that is, until I managed to get job as an inspector.

And whilst I was doing my inspection work, my mind was working overtime as I considered my future and the need to pay for the mortgage, not to mention the growing family and the roof for which I had no money.

And then the penny dropped as in the notion that, if I could build up a business from virtually nothing, I should be able to do the same for myself, which I did by establishing a business plan that was based on borrowed money.

The plan began with my working as a nightshift supervisor in a furniture company, which allowed me to do my marketing during the day, which led to my getting the first decent order and the beginning of my own business.

From here, I went to the bank with every subsequent order, where they would lend me enough money to complete the order, after which I had to return the money with interest, and so the business plan unravelled in due course.

I was soon in a position to buy a second hand car in the form of a two door, hard top, vinyl roof, V8 engine, copper/bronze metallic finished Valiant 777 series with low mileage and air conditioning, which I really enjoyed.

After all, I had been driving little clapped out VWs until then, which didn't have any guts unless they were going down hill with the wind from behind, which certainly didn't apply to this little head turner with power to burn.

I was also doing most of my selling in Sydney where I sometimes went to Kings Cross to watch a strip show or two, one of which involved a naked girl who was smearing iridescent coloured creams all over her body.

And as I slowly made my way to the stage, I ended up close enough to get her attention with a handful of coloured creams on my face and partially on my shirt, which I ended up having to explain to my wife back home.

Well, you see, they use colour coding on the greases in the factory so they can tell them apart, that's why!

That was my story, and I seemed to have got away with it until I took my wife to the same strip club a year later, when she made a connection between the act on the stage (and same girl) and the 'grease' on my shirt.

All in all, I was always close to the edge as I slowly built up the business with the help of my wife, neighbours and friends, one of which allowed me to use a portion of his factory and some of the equipment after hours.

On one occasion, I had to finish an urgent job to be delivered to Sydney on the next day, for which I worked through the night until Saturday, where we were booked into a flash hotel as an anniversary treat.

Unfortunately, I slept through much of day and the evening where we apparently had a fantastic meal and enjoyed a show, none of which I seemed to remember the next day, such is life in a one man venture.

And just when I considered myself on my way to a successful and growing business, I received a call from 'The Arsehole from Hell' informing me of the need to talk to him, if I knew what was good for me.

And so I took up his offer to meet him and his wife at his home, where he informed me that my little venture was about to come to an end due to the simple fact that, if he didn't finish me off now, I could be doing him a lot of damage.

Needless to say, I was outraged as I reminded him that I was the one who got him into this business, and so it was my turn in the knowledge that there was enough business to keep all of us busy for the foreseeable future.

I then inquired with respect to his plan of putting me out of business, to which he answered with a stupid grin on his face that he had more money than me, which he was going to employ as a strategy to destroy me.

He ten continued to outline his plan which was to take me to court for taking advantage of the skills and contacts applying to his particular mode of operation, to which I informed him that I was the originator of the skills etc.

I know that, he replied, and I don't expect to win, but I am going to continue with my harassing you in court and underquoting you below cost price until you run out money or customers, whichever comes first.

Well, that took the cake, and so I stormed out of his house vowing to fight him for as long as I had the energy and the money to do so, which lasted about a year, after which I was broke to the point where I had to sell my car.

I ended up selling whatever was left of the business at a price that reflected nothing like its real value, but ten again, I was fed up with the dirty practices associated with the running of a business, where the evil ruled the day.

In fact, it was on more than one occasion that I developed a clever solution to a problem that was then followed up with an expensive prototype so as to demonstrate the design concept, whilst in the possession of the client.

And then I was informed that I was unsuccessful with my bid, whilst my design was made by a competitor who was a crony of whoever did the purchasing; I wouldn't be surprised if he got a kickback or some other inducement.

It was soon after, that I noticed an ad for a production engineer with a Fastener Company, where I ended up working for the next 6 years or so reporting to a German boss by the name of Joe, who I got on well with.

This was partially due to the fact that he was always biting off more than he could chew, in which case he relied on his staff to get him out a scrape, which was my particular skill and value to him that continued for years.

I remember on one occasion, we were tooling up for a toggle bolt, which needed to be assembled by a group of employees who were willing to take work home at a particularly low rate of pay, which they didn't seem to mind.

The trouble was, nobody knew how to assemble the three part product, and so the boss issued a challenge to whoever was willing to make a name for him or herself, which was like a red rag to a bull as far as I was concerned.

Well, it didn't take me long to win the challenge, which impressed the boss no end as he continued to feed me with more and more complex challenges, which I managed to address with an ease that even surprised me.

On another occasion, the lady supervisor of the in-house assembly and packing section asked me if I could help her with her homework consisting of a manual device to cut plastic tubing to a given length, one at a time.

I informed her that, if I was to help her through the company, all gains would be absorbed by the company, in which case she would be left with less work and less money, which was not exactly what she had in mind.

I offered to help her personally for a bottle of whiskey, to which she agreed as I was planning for a cutting concept that involved the purchase of a second hand sewing machine and a few other hand made bits and pieces.

And when everything was finished, I made an appointment with her at her house, where I would duly demonstrate my little ripper that took no effort to operate whilst it was spewing the plastic bits out at an astronomical rate.

When I worked out the hourly rate this lady was about to earn, I realized that she would be getting paid more than the prime minister at the time, which was nevertheless only an hour or so per week whilst she watched television.

There was other 'home work' to be had in the form of a 'Dynabolt' assembly consisting of a bolt with a tapered head, one or two sleeves, a washer and a nut, the most time consuming part of which was the screwing of the nut.

The bulk of the assembly was subcontracted to a workshop of disabled people who had a real problem with the screwing of the nut, as their hands and fingers were often not as they should, which soon came to my notice.

And so I designed a tray with a hole in the middle, below which I mounted a small motor with a fixture designed to receive the nut and washer, which would then rotate whilst the operator pressed the bolt and sleeve onto it.

The screwing would then come to a timely stop as the nut was lifted from the friction part on the revolving fixture, which really impressed the disabled to the point where they gave me a standing ovation, which really humbled me.

The supervisor told me thereafter that the disabled operators were not allowed to use motorised equipment up to that point, in which case my gadget represented a bit of a break through, which they really appreciated.

I was starting to get a bit of a reputation when my boss informed me of a supplier that was charging them excessive prices for their automatic screw gun 'screw belts' as in a set of 100 screws embedded in a plastic carrier.

As he showed me the sample screw belt, he asked me if I could build a machine that could produce the same belt contained 'our' screws, at a development cost of $5,000 maximum (1974) and within three months from now.

Stupid me said there and then "No Worries", which is Aussie for "I haven't got a clue how I am going to do this at such a ridiculous price and within such an impossible time frame", but then again, I was a

Aries who *"may consider itself infallible and become absorbed by its intellect",* as I did at the time.

When I asked my boss about the alternatives, he said that they could buy a machine from Germany for $100,000 or continue to be 'screwed' by the supplier, which really cheered me up with respect to their confidence in me.

Anyway, I asked for a toolmaker to be 100% allocated to me and be given access to the obsolete machinery store, where I discovered a machine that allowed me to use my design concept without having to start from scratch.

Cut a long story short, I managed to finish the machine on time and on budget, which seemed to impress the 'Big Boss' and owner as he witnessed the machine in operation with words like "It is so bloody simple".

To some degree, I was digging a hole for myself as the projects became bigger and better until I came undone when they asked me to design a semi automatic machine for assembling the Dynabolt range.

Not that I failed in my design, but rather in my anticipation of the 100% quality requirement of the components that were automatically fed into the machine, in which case a single defect would stop the machine.

This became obvious when I demonstrated the machine to the 'Big Boss' together with a few of the top brass who were eagerly awaiting the 'cash cow' that was going to do away with all the subcontracting of the assembly.

And then the machine stopped, upon which I quickly identified the cause as a bent washer, which I held up triumphantly as a sign of my faith in my own design, but there was more to come, like a stoppage every ten seconds.

At first I thought that somebody had tried to sabotage my management presentation, but I soon realized that the upstream production areas were unable to provide me with perfect sleeves, spacers, bolts, washers and nuts.

And so the Dynabolt Assembly project was scrapped, which taught me one hell of a lesson that was to help me later in life when I made a living as a 'Quality Management Consultant', but I am getting ahead of myself.

There was worse to come as the 'Big Boss' appointed a new works manager who was renowned for his cost cutting ways and generally lack of communication and regard for the little people of the organization.

This led to a change in management structure as my boss Joe left the company, and the maintenance manager became my new boss, who hated my guts as he thought that 'he' should have designed all machines.

As a consequence, he sat me in a corner and gave me some clerical work whilst he treated me with contempt, which left me once again in a frustration mode as I contemplated my future with the company on the whole.

In the meantime, Joe heard about my situation and so he asked to meet him in a pub where he offered me a job in an automotive supply company where he was the general manager, and there were plenty of challenges.

Need less to say, I accepted the job there and then, which caused a bit of a stir at my place of work, whilst my boss couldn't wipe the smile off his face, the slimy bastard, who thereafter gave me the worst send-off I have ever had.

And whilst he was deeply religious, he couldn't help telling the folks on my send off what a lousy engineer I was and how little they were going to miss me, which fortunately didn't make much of an impression on the folks.

Much to my surprise, the managing director called me into his office and thanked me for all my excellent work whilst he handed me an envelope with a cheque inside as a sign of his appreciation – what a man.

And when I opened the envelope in the privacy of my corner, I started to feel like a prostitute as the amount was an insult for all the work I had put in, much of which was in my own time and on my own volition

By now I had developed a new perspective in life whereby I was now looking out for myself and my family, as a good situation in any workplace could easily change in an instant, as I kept on finding out time and again.

Anyway, back to good old Joe who let me loose on a challenge associated with one of their major products, which was costing too much to produce as it was based entirely on the availability of two or more 'strong' men.

The product consisted of a 'Loop-link' as in the elongated link at the top of your safety belt which is fixed to the frame of the car, the critical aspect of which was associated with the absolute smoothness of the inner edges.

That is, if there was a slightest imperfection, the seat belt would fray as it travelled back and forth through, or in and out of, the Loop-link, and in that laid the challenge which equally applied to all other producers in the world.

As far as the cost relating to the manual operation and the 'strongman' requirement was concerned, the link started off with a blank rod that was fed into a jig, after which the operator had to manually bend the rod, one end at a time.

In doing so, each bend was somewhat past the right angle but not as far as necessary for the next operation, the reason for this had to do with the need to remove the link from the jig after every consecutive bending operation.

This was the kind of challenge I really enjoyed, and whilst I cannot tell you my solution, I ended up creating an automatic machine that only had to be refilled with the blank rods, which put a couple of workers out of a job.

The automotive industry was always very active when it came to their communication with the supply companies and the need to produce better and cheaper products, much of which came from the mother country Japan.

And so one day our company was informed of the need to send an engineer to Japan and to visit the major car companies as well as some of their key suppliers, in which case I was chosen in the autumn of 1979.

Apart from me, there was also the big boss who happened to be of the persuasion that everybody had to wear a tie all of the time, or else, which brings me back to my birth, where the umbilical cord was wrapped around my neck.

The experience reared its ugly head in the form of a rash on the neck whenever I had to wear a tie later on in life, which I had explained to Joe and he had given me an exemption, which the big boss had then overruled.

Such was the mentality of many a chief executive at the time, which didn't help with the morale of the team, nor did it bring out the best in the employees, many of which were just biding their time or looking for employment elsewhere.

Having been there and done that too many times already without being able to find an ideal place of work, I decided to see my doctor about the problem, upon which he wrote me a certificate of psychological damage at the time of birth.

To cut a long story short, the big boss begrudgingly accepted my certificate under the condition that I was to wear a tie whenever we had important visitors and I was involved with the discussions, to which I begrudgingly agreed.

As I didn't have a current Visa, I had to go through the rigmarole of applying for a new Visa, which involved the supply of two personal pictures or mug shots, which I requested to be paid for by the company.

As far as I was concerned, any expenses on my behalf relating to the overseas trip should be paid for by the company, regardless of whether I could have used the Visa for my own purposes thereafter, or not.

And then the big boss found out about my request and reluctantly obliged by consenting to pay for two of the pictures which normally came in a batch of four, and so I was left to pay for the remainder without having a need for it.

Well, I could feel my blood boiling as I was starting to get a bad feeling about my trip to Japan and forthcoming isolation with a person who was always counting his pennies whilst the pounds went out the window.

Anyway, I got on the plane and set next to the boss who was about to become a six week long pain in the arse in more ways than I dare telling you about. (No—he was not homosexual)

I remember sitting in his hotel room night after night whilst we were drinking whisky with our designated Japanese guide, the purpose of which was to save money rather than experiencing the real Japan.

At the same time, he was running down the Australian worker as he admired the Japanese willingness to work beyond the call of duty, which we observed repeatedly during out visits to the various suppliers of components.

On one occasion, the supply company had invested in the latest technology relating to the operator safety of a Stamping Press, where the ram would stop in midstream if somebody got his hand in the way of the tool.

On the next day, we witnessed the cheaper version of the concept whereby the operator was strapped to the press by way of two cufflinks with strings to the safety mechanism which would stop the ram, if necessary.

In the meantime the boss kept on with his routine of drinking whisky and degrading the Aussie worker to the point where I just couldn't take any more, and so I told him in no uncertain terms that it was all 'his' fault.

After all, according to my experience, "You get out what you put in", and this is where I disagreed with my boss on the simple notion that the Japanese were 'really' looking after their employees, and he wasn't.

With that, the boss took one look at me as he turned to the Japanese guide and replied that I was a typical example of the Australian employee, as I was obviously not of the same calibre as my Japanese counterparts.

From thereon, we did not have any more whisky in his hotel room, as we were now walking the streets to find a Sony Walkman for his son, the nature of which also began to get on my nerves before long.

To be specific, he had been making inquiries from the moment we stepped off the plane in Tokyo with the intent of buying the absolute cheapest Walkman in the whole of Japan, and we still had a long way to go.

In the process, he kept on asking the same stupid questions over and over again like "How much is it, is that the cheapest price, how does it work, is it guaranteed, how long does it last, and does it come with a cassette?"

I was no longer willing to go into the shop with him as I was ready to kill him, the desire to do so grew with every day, the culmination of which came after he suggested we walk into this red light district just to have a look.

Well, the little look was soon followed by a little more probing like getting into this girly bar, which reminded me of my first trip to the red light district in Hamburg, and fair enough, the routine was exactly the same.

And when I asked the man at the bar with respect to the current size of our bill, it was also astronomical just like in Hamburg, and so I proposed to the boss that we better get out of here before we spent all our money.

With that, he suggested I pay his and my the bill with the comment that I should not expect him or the company to reimburse me as I had taken him to this house of ill repute against his will, and that is when I killed him. (in my mind)

From hereon, I refused to talk to him as we continued with our trip and I was looking forward to getting back home, whilst he continued to go from shop to shop to inquire about the cheapest Walkman in the whole of Japan.

Finally, it was time to leave and get on the plane, when the boss suddenly realized that he still hadn't bought this bloody Sony Walkman, and so he rushed off the plane to the nearest shop where he paid the absolute top dollar.

How this man ever managed to become a self-made millionaire is beyond me, and I wouldn't be surprised to find out that he amassed his fortune at the expense of the Australian workers who had a gutful of people like him.

When we got back, my boss Joe called me into his office and began to ask me what had happened in Japan, as the Big Boss was running me down in no uncertain terms, which surprise him as he knew me better.

And when I explained to him the matter of the two pictures, the whisky sessions and the red light district experience, he understood exactly where I was coming from as he assured me that all would be paid for by the company.

I was then asked to apply my newly acquired knowledge to the benefit of the company, which I did in the form of a handful of proposals that could have saved the company millions, and I was keen to get cracking.

And then one week went past after another, during which I frequently inquired about my proposals, only to be told that there were too many problems that needed to be fixed, and so I should be patient and wait my turn.

After three months of the same rhetoric, I had a gutful and so I perused the paper for another job, which got me onto this personnel consultant and a queue of applicants that reminded me of my application in Bremen before I emigrated.

These guys were all dolled up in suits and ties with shiny shoes and manicured fingernails reading 'The Financial Review', whilst I was sitting there in my shirt without a tie, thinking that I didn't have a chance in hell.

As it happened, the position was with another fastener manufacturer who had actually supplied the screw belts for which I had built a machine at the other company, and so there was no contest when it came to my getting the job.

My reputation must have filtered through to the management who threw me straight into the biggest challenge relating to the problems associated with their Self-drilling screws, the production of which I was not familiar with.

And so I applied myself to the best of my knowledge, when I realized that there were basic problems with the process, the specifications, some of the clamping tools, the measuring instruments and the process maintenance.

I thought a little and then came up with my plan, which was to take two operators who had never worked on these machines before and then run a nightshift, which the company was not operating at the time.

After a bit of a hassle with management, I was granted my wish, and so I was ready to embark on another challenge that was potentially going to make or break me, which had never bothered me before.

As it happened, I applied some of the concepts and principles that I had learnt in Japan, which were broadly defined under the heading of "Total Quality Control", which was also making its way into the western countries.

One of the features of the Japanese approach had to do with its participative management style, where the "Team Members" developed a type of "Team Spirit" whilst they were engaging in the pursuit of a common goal.

Cut a long story short, after a period of 3 months, the two boys and I were producing near perfect product during the nightshift with new specifications, measuring instruments, clamping tools and process maintenance.

And so the concept was introduced to the day shift, as I returned to my post as a production engineer and trained the operators in the new procedures, which turned out to be a real winner in the qualitative and quantitative sense.

When the American boss got to hear about this, he suggested that I should go to Germany and show the Germans how to suck eggs – the Aussie way, which led to my going to Dortmund in December/ January in 1981.

As my boss was reluctant to let me go, I suggested to him that I work through my Christmas holidays in Germany providing I was allowed to take my wife and three kids with me in exchange for working without any pay.

The American boss agreed, and so we set off to visit the old country for the first time after 22 years of absence, during which we mixed business with pleasure as I worked in Dortmund and also in Hamburg, where my aunt lived.

I continued in my role as a production engineer when I was given another chance to go to Europe in 1983, where I was to present our ongoing commitment to the "Total Quality Control" or TQC concepts.

This time, I was travelling alone as I went to Spain, Germany and England, where I was to present a two day seminar on the virtues of 'Right the First Time – Every Time' production technology, which I was looking forward to.

My first port of call was Barcelona, where I was to do my presentation for the Spanish and Italian management representatives, who made me exceedingly welcome and feel like a king or a saviour from 'Down Under'.

In reality, they used my visit as an excuse to have expensive lunches and dinners until late into the night, as we frequented places where Columbus was known to hang out, and many more, but who was I to complain?

I also met a Spanish importer of clothing on the plane to Barcelona who offered to show me the town together with his girlfriend, which they did on my day off where I experienced the Spanish hospitality from another angle.

That evening, the pair took me to where the action was on a mile long strip by the name of La Rambla, where I witnessed a myriad of free street entertainment, bars, nightclubs and restaurants, just to mention a few.

We were cruising down the street at around 12 o'clock midnight when my friend pointed to a long queue of not so well dressed men who were progressing steadily towards this particular building, which had no advertising.

When I asked him about the significance, he informed me that the building was the local brothel where the girls not only dropped their pants after midnight, but also their prices to the point where 'everybody' could afford them.

At the same time, there was a big burly bloke standing next to each girl and, if the customer didn't get off within the allocate minute or two, he was simply ripped of the girl and thrown out the door, that's what I call a 'Quickie'.

The experience reminded me of the little old man with a walking stick in my hometown who was queuing up for his last leg-over, when he was refused the privilege to do so by the not so socially minded busty blond.

I was furthermore informed that La Rambla represented a divide between the underworld on one side, and the normal world on the other, and not ever to venture into the first, as I was sure as hell going to be murdered or robbed.

On a more pleasant note, the Spanish seemed to have an entirely different outlook to us, as they regularly had long lunches, followed by Spanish Brandy that is strong enough to leave you in a state of Zombie for the rest of the day.

All in all, I left Barcelona with the best memories of the people, the places, the hospitality and the hangovers, which was largely due to the Spanish Brandy, but then again, "When in Spain—Do as the Spanish Do", Ole.

My next destination was Hamburg where I experienced the German hospitality, which might have been a bit more restrained when it came to the long lunches, but left no stone unturned when it came to the nightlife.

Apart from the incredible eating experiences, I was also re-introduced to the 'Reeperbahn', where we ended up in this particular famous night spot, strip club or sex show that was almost more than I could handle.

The highlight was in the form of an old bloke, (and he was definitely old) who was in bed whilst this nurse tried to breathe some life into him by way of stripping off and performing a number of weird and wonderful exercises.

This seemed to get the old bloke into the mood as he got out of bed and proceeded to mount the nurse on a small revolving table which was barely big enough to give him a footing for what was about to come.

Cut a long story short, (sorry about that) he made love to her whilst the table rotated at a fair rate of knots, which was an acrobatic performance in its own right, not to mention the final outcome of this extraordinary act.

On the other hand, I will mention the fact that he definitely delivered the goods as he proceeded to cover the nurse with his sperm; and to think that he was an old bloke who was doing this act every night, 7 days a week.

I was going to ask him what it was that made him so potent in the downstairs department, but I didn't get the chance as we moved on to the next event, after which my memory is starting to leave me for some reason.

On the next day, it was off to London town where I was treated with the best hospitality a Brit could muster, which began that evening in a pub where the well known TV personality Michael Parkinson was usually drinking.

And fair enough, there he was at the bar sipping a warm beer, as you would in Britain, which was something I was yet to get used to for a day or two during my stay in town, much of which was spent in pubs.

I had managers from all over Europe who had converged on 'Monkey Island' in London where I was to deliver my address, which I did in the most boring but accurate fashion an engineer could possibly come up with.

When I was informed of my mixed performance that night by non-other than the Big Boss from America who suggested that I should be a little more interactive and throw in a joke here and there, I had a sleepless night.

On the next day, I delivered my message in a story about a farm hand who was stalked by his female boss, which allowed me to incorporate the key statistical aspects relating to the objective of "Right the First Time – Every Time".

I had previously told the story during a night of drinking with the Melbourne management team in one of the local hotels, where we all took part in a joke telling competition and I was intent on winning for my team of drunken idiots.

I was using a mixture of English and Benny Hill style broken German with gestures that didn't need to be explained when it came to the farm hand and the size of his 'you know what', which won us the competition.

In principle, the story was based on the use simple statistical tools involving:

a) the Cause & Effect Analysis, which the boss lady was using to list 'all' the possible causes relating to her sexual frustration as a farmer without a husband or a lover, which had led to her interest in the farm hand;

b) the Pareto Chart, which she was using to identify the single greatest cause of all the listed causes, the nature of which happened to be the size of the male's genitalia, which she couldn't tell until after the event;

c) the Correlation Chart, which she used to establish a correlation between a feature that could be easily identified and assessed as a representative feature and size of the genitalia, without having to go to bed first;

d) the Research and Development Plan, which she used to establish her data as a basis for the potential correlation between the size of the head, body height, nationality, facial feature or shoe size, just to mention a few.

And whilst she spent a lot of time doing her 'research', she finally found a near perfect correlation between the size of the shoe and the size of the male genitalia, which had led to her obsession with the farm hand.

Anyway, her persistence paid off as she called the farm hand into her kitchen whilst she offered him a beer, which he was more than willing to accept, after which she lured him into her bedroom, which he also accepted.

Cut a long story short, (sorry again for that) there was a great amount of satisfaction on both sides, upon which the lady boss reached into her purse and handed the farm hand a $100 bill, to which he replied with excitement:

"Wow, this is getting better by the minute, but to what do I owe this treatment of beer, sex, and now this money, have you lost your mind, lady?"

With that she turned to leave with words like "You better buy yourself a bigger pair of shoes "cause the ones you are wearing must be killing you!"

I couldn't help thinking about the application of the basic statistical tools in this manner, as the emotional side of the lovemaking had entire gone out the window, but then again, the results spoke for themselves.

It so happened, my audience was no longer bored as they gave me a standing ovation for my weird performance whilst remembering the key aspects associated with a "Right the First Time – Every Time" outcome.

On my return, the news of my little presentation and success had got back to the company, which seemed to worry my production engineering manager as he put me into a corner and gave me some clerical work to do.

Having been there and done that before at the other fastener company, I proceeded to talk to the general manager who understood where I was coming from, as he knew the personality of the manager in question.

He then questioned me with respect to my expertise in the Japanese Total Quality Control practices, which was becoming a bit of a buzz word in the industry, and my efforts so far seemed to align with that philosophy.

Well, I simply told him what I knew and had learnt in Japan, after which I was appointed the new quality manager and given a car as a form of appreciation and means to visit clients and perform other business functions.

I was also promised a substantial raise in my salary in line with my new responsibility and the expectations that go with the management position, the payment of which I was looking forward to over the next month or three.

And when nothing was said, I queried the general manager with respect to his promise, to which he informed me that they had already paid for my family to go to Germany, whilst forgetting the fact that I had worked for nothing.

How did I get myself into these situations, where my eagerness to please others was being exploited by some smart arse boss who thought I was dumb enough to fall for this type of mismanagement of the human resources.

Shortly after this, my old mate Joe rang me up and informed me that he needed a good quality manager and he had heard about my success with the fastener company, which couldn't have come at a better time.

And so I gave notice as I was making my way back into an industry where quality was paramount, whilst the big penny pinching boss was questioning the wisdom of my return to the scene of my earlier crime, as he put it.

I was starting to broaden my experience in the quality management field as I was helped by such companies as Ford Australia who was running seminars on process control, Zero Defect, problem solving and similar subjects.

And whilst I was doing my best to create a new attitude towards quality management and the importance of doing the job 'Right the First Time – Every Time", there was an element that I had virtually no control over.

That is, I remember on this one occasion, we were making Gear Shift Assemblies that were equipped with green globes, the purpose of which was to signify the correct gear position relating to a given application.

It so happened, the store had run out of green globes to the point where the production run had to be stopped, which was then presented to the production manager who promptly instructed them to use red globes instead.

Try and imagine the scenario happening in a Traffic Light assembly line, where the green light is actually red, and so the cars would stop until somebody informed the traffic authorities, if it ever got that far.

Fortunately, it didn't get that far with the customer who demanded an explanation, for which there was none other than to blame some innocent assembly worker, whilst the production manager got off Scott free.

Soon after, we had another complaint about the very same product, whereby the gearshift operation was deemed exceedingly stiff, which made it difficult to operate, and so I was called in to get us out of the mess.

My instructions were to do whatever I could to prevent a recall, which would have cost the company an arm and a leg, which left me with no other option than to apply my natural ability to tell a story that may not always be true.

After investigating the problem area relating to an oversize plastic bearing bush that was causing the friction, I came up with the story of a 'cold flow' phenomenon or material creep once the product had been installed.

As the customer couldn't disproof that phenomenon in relation to their problem, we were left off the hook, after which I was proclaimed as "The best Quality Manager we have ever had", and to hell with all this TQC crap.

On another occasion, there was a batch of faulty components for another customer, which was passed to the production manager who, in turn passed it to the general manager Joe, who passed it onto the penny pinching Big Boss.

Not a problem, said the Big Boss, as he came up with the perfect answer consisting of a handful of good parts at the top of the drum used for the delivery, whilst the bad parts were at the bottom – problem solved.

And then the drum was turned upside down at the customer end, where the inwards goods inspection people proceeded to check the delivery from a quality angle, and it was then that the conspiracy was discovered.

How do you deal with this type of "Top Down" wilful mismanagement of the single most important factor within the entire spectrum of stakeholders in the business – the customer, who can quickly make or break you?

This had not been an isolated case, as I found out by the huge pile of rejects behind the factory, some of which had to do with the recalls of cars, for which the company had been insured if and when this may occur.

But then again, no insurance company is prepared to pay for the customer's repeated failure to provide product "Right the First Time – Every Time", which was reflected in the one million dollar excess of the insurance contract.

Not surprisingly, Joe hired a consultant who had previously been a quality manager with the company some years before and was now working for himself, which suited me as we got on well and also respected each other.

He even invited me to speak at some of his seminars, where I started to develop a liking for this sort of thing, as my ego or esteem need got the better of me on the odd occasion, as I was destined to do as an Aries.

Considering the quality management concept had become a hot potato to the Australian automotive industry first and foremost, there was plenty of demand for this type of expertise, of which there was little at the time.

And so I wasn't surprised when the consultant offered me the opportunity of becoming an independent consultant, or Sole Trader, who was getting the bulk of his work from one source, as in his consulting company.

That night, my wife and I discussed the matter, which led to my resignation with the penny pinching boss, which I duly announced to Joe the next day together with an apology for letting him down in the hour of need.

He smiled at me as he informed me that, he too, had a gutful of the big boss and his penny pinching ways and also given his own notice, whilst he was looking forward to running a supermarket which he had purchased.

I was looking forward to my first assignment as I was given the opportunity to spend one week at a time with the management teams of Ansett Freight Express in Perth, Brisbane, Sydney, Adelaide, Albury and Melbourne.

I was given a pile of Overhead Transparencies and a Video Tape that I somehow had to convert into a meaningful five day seminar, which was further supported by my having to attend the nightly drinking sessions.

The 'Cultural Conversion' was introduced by the CEO with words like "We are spending a shit-load of money, so you better pull your f-—--——g finger out", which went down like a led balloon when it came to its powers of motivation.

And from hereon, I was pushing shit up hill as the 'Team Members' saw me as the objective of their lack of motivation to listen and learn the basic concepts associated with Total Quality Control, five days eight hours a day.

On Friday night, I would fly back to Melbourne and on Sunday fly to the next "Mission Impossible" in another state or town, which was more than I could handle, as I was only human and ready to give the game away.

On one occasion in Melbourne, I had used the example of the statistical tools and the lady farmer who was looking for a 'Right the First Time – Every Time' outcome, which seemed to go down particularly well.

At the end, the leader of the team presented me with a huge pair of shoes, which he followed up with the words "You are one of the biggest pricks we have come across in a long while', which made me feel really proud.

After having 'converted' the various states, the boss set up a seminar with some of the top brass in a convention centre where we were supposed to explain the next stage in the planned cultural conversion process.

As to my part, I was honing in on the interaction problem and the authoritarian approach, which had produced the opposite effect to what I was hoping to achieve, in which case the CEO represented the root of the problem.

Talk about David and Goliath, as I found out after the seminar when the CEO requested that I should no longer attend their seminars and, by the way "I suggest you fire the little bastard who tried to make a fool out of me."

I then realized that I had not only overstepped the mark, but I was also in the wrong game when it came to my strengths, the key to which lied in my ability to solve complex problems *"whilst being the boss most of the time".*

From hereon, I was lingering in my capacity to please the clients and the boss who was handing out the contracts to the point where, after having been a Sole Trader for a year or so, I was told I was no longer required.

I was shattered as I had little chance of getting back into the industry, considering I was almost 50 and had been changing jobs too many times to be considered a worthy employee who would stick around until retirement.

And then I received a call from a mate who had recommended me to this specialized consulting company who was about to open a quality management service as an extension of its computer based technology.

Luckily, they were not aware of my past as they offered me a position that was to see me through for another year, when they decided to close that part of their business, despite of the excellent money I was earning them.

That is, I had been given the job of implementing a Quality Assurance System to the International Standards ISO 9001 for manufacturing and design with a large company, which took me close to a year to complete.

And whilst I learned a lot about the standards in principle, I was making my boss a lot of money as I was an employee of the company and getting superannuation and 50% of anything I earned over $50.000 a year.

Why they abandoned this growth market was beyond me, as I was perfectly suited for this type of work, but then again, they knew nothing about quality management as they made all of their money in the computer industry.

Anyway, I was looking forward to my bonus and superannuation at the end of my time, when they informed me that they couldn't fulfil their obligations as the company was in financial trouble, which was a big fat lie.

As it happened, the company was owned by an accountant and his son who had combined their business acumen with two minor partners, who they embezzled over the next couple of years, like they had embezzled me.

Fortunately, the two partners found out about this, after which they took the company to court, where they were convicted and sent to jail, which made me feel a little better about my loss of money at my own departure.

I was now looking back on my life, wondering what would have become of me if I had stayed in Germany, where the authoritarian management style might have interfered with my desire to think and act outside the square.

And then I remembered the promise by the 'One Pound at a Time' boss who had promised me the top job, which most likely would have eventuated as I found out not so long ago when I ran into my junior draftsman.

That is, I was at a seminar when this fellow walked up to me and said "Remember me?" and I recognized him as the boy I hired to take over my drawing responsibility, who was also the current CEO of a thriving business.

"This could have been your job!" he explained, and I was a little bit unsure at the time until I looked back over my own life and my idiosyncrasy, which would not have lent itself for this type of predictable career and life style.

On the other hand, I wouldn't have been in the pickle I was right now, which brings me to 'The Arsehole from Hell' who I looked up many years after my departure, upon which he said "I am surprised to see you after what I did to you!"

It so happened, he had done me a real favour as I was becoming so involved with the growth of my business at that stage that I had no time for my family, as I was working day and night creating a prison for myself.

By the same token, I would not have got out of that kind of madness unless somebody pulled the carpet from under my feet, for which I had to thank him despite his bizarre personality and behaviour towards me.

And as we chatted about the old days, he told me about his near death experience when he suspected that his wife and three kids were trying to poison him, and so he called them together to divulge one of his evil plans.

That is, he accused them outright that they were trying to kill him so that they could lay their hands on his money and, unless they admitted to this and delivered the key conspirator, he would write them out of his will.

And to the truth they got, as they sent him to (no, not a psychiatrist) a homeopath who quickly identified the root of his problem in the form of his Pituitary gland which secretes nine hormones that regulate homeostasis.

After that, his family fell apart as he was slowly recovering, which eventually led to his wife divorcing him, as I found out a couple of years later when I thought I might drop by so see how the old bastard was going.

And as I entered the office, this busty blonde who couldn't smile unless you gave her an envelope with an undisclosed amount of money inside walked up to me and inquired about the nature of my business.

Just then, the boss walked in and greeted me whilst he introduced me to his new wife, who he had only married just recently, after which we went into his office where we chatted for a while before I left and said good bye.

A couple of years later, my curiosity got the better of me as I dropped in unannounced, only to be informed by the boss's youngest daughter who was now running the place that her father was in India looking for 'Enlightenment'.

And then she enlightened 'me' with respect to the evil stepmother who they all hated, whilst she told me that this lady (of the night) had in fact been a masseuse, as she put it, but they were now happily divorced, thank God.

She then elaborated by telling me about the divorce, which cost her father a cool 1.7 million dollars, after which the rest of the family refused to have anything to do with him whilst she, the youngest daughter, was left to care for him.

In doing so, he had contaminated her marriage to the point where she ended up divorced with three children who were now trying to run the business as best as they could, whilst the evil bastard was living it up overseas.

For a minute, I could see myself being in her position if I had persisted in my job, where my marriage would have eventually got in the way of his bottomless greed and evil doings, and I would have been left to pick up the pieces.

And then I remembered my time with my mate Joe who had bought himself a supermarket, which seemed to revive his spirit until he developed cancer and died before he could enjoy the fruit of a lifetime of hard work.

I also found out that our penny pinching boss had been caught by his wife with a prostitute, or girlfriend, which had severely affected their marriage which lasted for a couple of years until, he too, died early from cancer.

Whilst I am on the subject of dying, my father died prematurely in 1976 when he had become a jeweller who was starting to make a name for himself to the point where he was about to have an exhibition of his work.

In doing so, he was working day and night up to a week before the exhibition when he suffered a major heart attack, which he shrugged off by immersing himself in an alternating hot and cold bathing process.

After that, he returned to his preparation for the exhibition during which he suffered three more heart attacks, which he dealt with in the same manner until he got to the point where he was taken to a hospital for treatment.

As it happened, he had been his own worst enemy by not going to the hospital straight away, where they could have saved his heart that was now beyond repair, which gave him only a few more weeks to live.

After his death, my mother moved in with my younger sister, where she died soon after as she wanted to be with dad, who might have been a bit of a monster here and there, but then again, who is perfect—except for you and me?

Unfortunately, my younger sister also died soon after when she was still minding her three teenage children, which left one hell of a hole in the family, considering my older sister had emigrated to Canada with her husband.

This brings me to my brother who had eventually left the navy to get married and start a family, which he did in the same suburb as my younger sister, where they had three children and a good life to look forward to.

That is, until the pair got involved in a swinging habit which led to the point where the neighbour had got to hear about it, upon which he inquired whether they could do a bit of neighbourly swinging during a barbeque.

When my brother asked him whether his wife was OK with this, he informed him that she was more than willing and waiting for my brother next door, and so the wheels kept on turning until my brother entered the bedroom.

What was about to happen reminded me of the time when my brother urged me to climb the balcony in Caulfield next to the racecourse, where I kissed the wrong girl and she became hysterical and called for her mother.

And whilst it was not her mother the woman was calling for, she called for the police who duly arrested my brother for the attempted rape of a non-consenting mother of three who had no idea about her husband's arrangement.

Well, that stifled the relationship to the point where they sold the house and decided to live in a caravan until they could find a block in the country near Ballarat, prior to which they would live in a caravan park in the suburbs.

Everything seemed to be going smooth as they pulled the van through the streets, that is, until the car in front of them stopped suddenly and my brother tried to avoid running into the rear by swerving sharp to the left.

Unfortunately, this type of manoeuvre was beyond the design of the van, which duly overturned whilst spreading their belongings all over the road – what a mess.

Anyway, they eventually ended up living in Scarsdale near Ballarat, where they bought an old wooden house that was carted onto their block, where they lived happily for a number of years, more or less.

As you know, my brother had his ways, and his interpretation of the law was quite different to the ordinary citizen, which became more and more obvious as he consorted with some of his mates, one of which was Henry.

Henry had bought a block nearby and employed my brother to build him an A-frame house with all the trimmings that a bachelor could want, which my brother was good at and succeeded after six months or so.

And so Henry moved in and proceeded to enjoy the country life until he got bored and decided to start a printing business in Melbourne, for which he needed the money that was now tied up in his A-frame house.

Not a problem, he thought as he informed my brother of his plan, which involved Henry leaving his country home to live with friends, during which my brother would burn down the house which he had so lovingly built.

Well, the trick worked as Henry was now using the insurance money to start his printing business in Melbourne, which he ran for a couple of years until he got bored once again, and so he got in touch with my brother.

This time, the plan was for my brother to break into the factory and destroy the expensive printing presses and anything else of value, and then set the place on fire, which my brother took on without any problems.

Low and behold, the two of them got away with it once again, as the insurance company paid Henry out whilst he was scheming his next move in a society where everything is fair and well—until you get caught.

Strangely enough, they never did, which brings me to the next chapter in my brothers life as he eventually split up with his wife and moved to Queensland, where he made a name for himself in a Hippy Commune near Nambour.

He proceeded to build a beautiful house with carved posts and sloping ceilings which he shared with a few mates, whilst they engaged in a process of living off the land and the government, preferably the latter.

This is where my brother inevitable got involved with the drug trade, for which he was sent to Afghanistan to hollow out some furniture so that the dealers could hide their drugs from the customs on their way to Brisbane.

He was living with an ex-prostitute in the house whilst he was working in the area, some of which took him away for a week or two, which didn't bother him as he knew his girl was not going to let him down, or stray.

And then he finished his contract early, and so he came home un-announced to find his little prostitute in bed with his best mate, which didn't go down well, as this went against the code of "Honour amongst Thieves".

Soon after that, the house mysteriously burned down as my brother was frantically trying to save it, well, that was his version to the Police who were called in by his so called buddies who were now left without a home.

The next I heard of him was from a cell in the Nambour prison in which he stayed until the case came to court, where he was found innocent, and so he continued to live in another commune until he too died.

And again, the circumstances were shady, as my brother was contracted to build a 'Pole House', which was overlooking the foreshore and altogether magnificent once it was completed, after a year or more.

This takes me to the nature of my brother's remuneration in the form of a tax dodge by a retired pilot who was writing a book and deducting his wages by claiming that my brother was doing the proof reading, amongst others.

The house had progressed to the point where the poles had been erected and connected through the floor structure, which was now accessible from a walk way as part of the scaffolding, without there being any railing.

And that is where my brother came to grief when his chainsaw was found next to him after he fell off the scaffolding and onto his head, where he died instantly, much to the surprise of the owner who pleaded his innocence.

When I went to the area to investigate the circumstances, he informed me that my brother had been hired as a contractor who would supply all his tools and scaffolding, together with the necessary safety requirements and railing.

I was soon to find out about his shady dealings as he had provided all the gear whilst paying my brother a pittance, but it was too late to bring him back, and so I decided not to pursue the matter any further.

This brings me back to the here and now and my own situation without a job, as I took on an industrial sales position where I was on a commission basis without retainer or basic expenses as in petrol, which really drained my pockets.

I was basically going from factory to factory, which I did for about two weeks without selling anything when I came across this German fellow by the name of Heinz who chatted to me about his automatic inspection machine.

When I told him about my Quality Assurance background, he informed me that he was having a meeting the following day with a client (VDO) to discuss his need to comply with the company's specific quality requirements.

As it turned out, Heinz began his business by buying his first Swiss Style small diameter repetition turning machines from VDO, where he was working at the time as a machine operator or machine shop foreman.

The opportunity to do so was based on the new company policy to subcontract all machining processes and components that were outside the unique expertise associated with the instrument manufacturing industry.

Whilst this gave Heinz the opportunity to start his own business, he was quick to expand his clientele, as he didn't want to have all his eggs in one basket, which brings me back to his meeting with VDO the next day.

When I offered my assistance and the possibility of my joining him during his meeting, he agreed, and so I proceeded to impress the major customer with my expertise, which led to Heinz offering me my first contract.

The deal was that I would work for Heinz two days a week at a vastly reduced rate, which was just enough to see me through until I was able to secure another contract, and so I was off to a new start in my little life.

Considering Heinz's background as a German tradesman was always putting quality before quantity, I persuaded him to go slow whilst I was developing the perfect quality system, to which he agreed wholeheartedly.

At the same time, I saw an opportunity in developing a generic quality manual which could be sold on a DIY basis at a price well below the open-cheque arrangement with a consultant who then may or may not deliver the goods.

I was making good progress with my first assignment as a budding Quality Assurance Management consultant, when I had an accident that set me back for a while, as I sustained a cracked skull and a subdural haemorrhage.

I remember lying in the intensive care ward of the hospital with a huge headache, when the devil came to me with a big smile on his face as he said "I was wondering how long it would take you before you would join me?"

And whilst I was flattered by his somewhat premature welcome, I was thinking about my new direction in life and the fact that I still had a lot do before I was ready to join his rank and file in the warmest place on, or below, earth.

And so I declined his offer as I quickly recovered from my accident, which was nevertheless going to slow me down for some time to come yet, as my mate Heinz found out when I returned to his factory after two weeks.

As I was unable to drive, my wife delivered me in the morning, where I would crutch my way into office and proceed to do my work for two or three hours before I was unable to continue, and so my wife would pick me up again.

I must say, Heinz really showed me the stuff he was made off as he endured this type of 'consulting' practise for some time, until I managed to put in a whole day's work and also had my driving ban lifted – what a relief.

My lucky stars must have been with me as I discovered that Heinz was the president of the local Lions Club, where he recommended me to some of his business associates, which subsequently led to my getting more clients.

In the process, I was spreading my generic quality manual development of 20 elements and a generic Policy Manual over my expanding clientele to the point where I completed the entire ensemble in a matter of six months.

I then proceeded to sell the manual for a minimum of $3,600 each with the addition of my support for the implementation at $300 per half day, which led to more clients, some of which were recommended by Heinz.

Whilst I didn't think I owed Heinz anything other than giving me my first break, I paid him $500 for each successful recommendation, which seemed to please him no end, that is, until I thought I had shown enough gratitude.

Talk about the greed of the rich and powerful, which came to haunt me once again as Heinz told me that he hadn't received any money for his last recommendation, to which I replied that I was not obliged to pay him anything.

And this is where the whole thing began to turn into an ugly family affair as the daughter in law informed Heinz that I had been using her girlfriend to type up the manuals, the first couple of which were paid for by Heinz.

And whilst I was paying for everything from thereon, I gave Heinz a copy of the progressive manuals for nothing, which she was obviously not aware of, the scheming little bitch from hell who was now on a rampage.

That is, she promptly informed Heinz that 'he' owned the copyright of 'all' my materials from start to finish, which he swallowed hook, line and sinker as he informed my typist that I should have no more access to my files.

Considering I did not have a computer at the time, I was technically out of business – once again, and so I informed Heinz of the truth, after which he looked deeper into the matter and let me have my files back—how generous.

Not that I was relying on Heinz anymore as I was now selling my manual by direct mail to the prospective clients with a simple message reading "Efficient, Effective and Affordable", which ended up with a hundred sales plus after sales service.

Suddenly, I was back on top of the world as I was invited by the Moorabbin TAFE and Swinburne College to give seminars about the ISO 9000 Quality Management System and its implementation according to my manual.

In my wisdom, I contacted the Australian Standards in Melbourne, where I informed the top guy of my development, after which he got quite excited whilst he was keen to read my manual as a matter of keeping in the picture.

Soon after, I was assisting a company with the implementation of my manual when the director asked me if I was prepared to talk to the members of the 'Society of Manufacturing Engineers', or SME, to which I agreed happily.

He then asked me whether I could possibly arrange for the Australian Standards guy to give a short speech on the matter, to which I also agreed, as I had been given a positive feedback from the head man not so long ago.

He also suggested that my manual should be discreetly displayed during the meeting so as not to be seen as a promotion by the society, which made me very happy as I was counting the dollars that could come from this.

And then the evening arrived where I was eagerly waiting at the door to greet the Standards guy, but to no avail, and so I left it with that as I went inside to begin my presentation, which I was reasonably well prepared for.

What I was not prepared for was the fact that my Standards buddy and friend had purposely come late so as not to have to talk to me and inform me that he was going to boycott my presentation in the most evil fashion.

That is, he declared that a generic manual with or without the support of a trained consultant would never work, as every company represented a unique and different concept of manufacture and quality requirements.

When I asked him "How come the ISO 9000 System was designed to apply to every possible manufacturing scenario in a generic fashion", he declined to answer whilst he proceeded to sell his own consulting services.

And so the dream blew up in my face once again, as I had fallen for another "Arsehole from Hell", who seemed to see me coming from a long way off, and I was simply too naïve to know what was going on until it was too late.

Not to worry, I had more clients than I could handle at the time, which led to my advertising for other experienced consultants to sell my manual and to assist with the implementation, whilst I was to profit from the sale of the manual.

Well, it appeared as though the good guys were all booked up, as I found out when I contracted a couple of self proclaimed experts in the field of Quality Management, who turned out to be obnoxious and ill mannered.

I found this out when a prospective customer rang to inform me that my representative was a rude, pushy bastard who couldn't sell if he was giving the product away, and to be aware of his giving me a bad name in the industry.

And then there was this father and son combination of do-gooders who were deeply religious and keen to take my product on board with the assistance of a third person who was apparently without a job at the time.

I invited them to my house, where they proceeded to divide the anticipated profits from the sale of the manuals amongst themselves to the point where I was left with nothing, upon which they went into a group hug, the four of us.

And when I made them aware of their little oversight and the fact that I didn't want to have anything to do with their little scheme, they apologized before I threw them out of my house and suggested they never come back.

Shortly after that, I received a letter from the father who was all confused and apologetic as he quoted the Lord and his wholehearted commitment to the cause of helping other people, which obviously didn't include me.

As I was still feeling bad about my split with Heinz, I decided to drop by one day just say hello and see how he was going – no hard feelings.

Heinz seemed to be quite happy to see me as he invited me in, where I met up with his daughter in law and two sons whom he informed that I wanted to make friends, and so we happily forgave each other as we shook hands.

When I asked him how his quality system was coming along, he told me that the original goal had been achieved as in the requirements of his main customer at the time when I had originally met him and developed the system.

However, the market was now expecting the quality system to be certified by a third party, which would not only ensure the confidence of the Australian market, but also the overseas market, which he was now getting into.

It seemed like I was always knocking on his door just when he needed help, which suited me as I offered him my services and a special deal where I would work two days a week for as long as necessary, which he accepted.

I was also working for another company which had a similar history to Heinz, where the owner by the name of Hans had taken over the repetition turning machines from the first Fastener Company I had worked for.

And whilst this was before my time with the company, I had heard about him and his peculiar habit of adjusting the machine tools which, instead of using a spanner or a screw driver, he used to 'adjust' with a hammer blow, or two.

Hans had come from Hamburg and made good in Australia by working hard and taking risks, which worked out in his favour as he was now the owner of a thriving repetition engineering company, who was also expected to comply with the ISO 9000.

There is a particular story I would like to tell you about the obsession with the application of process control charts in the automotive industry above all, much of which was driven by the Ford Motor Company at the time.

And whilst the use of these charts reflected the Japanese concept of quality management and process control, the prerequisite to they application was based on the existence of a 'stable & predictable' process variability.

Hence, if a process was subject to wear, the concept could not be used as the desired outcome would either get progressively larger or smaller with wear, whilst the variability was nevertheless 'unstable but predictable'.

In doing so, the process would begin with the maximum wear allowance, after which the outcome would grow or shrink until the given tolerance had been taken up and the process was reset or the tool was resharpened.

Despite the obvious fact of an 'unstable but predictable' process variability associated with most of the machining involved, the automotive industry insisted that the suppliers used the charts and delivered them with the goods.

This had left the suppliers with two choices:

a) They could adjust the process constantly to obtain an artificial 'stable & predictable' process, in which case they would either lose their profit, or they would have to increase the price, which may then force them out of the market.

b) They could produce falsified control charts that were then sent with the goods, which would then be inspected at the customer end, where they served as the basis for their decision relating to the quality status of the product.

Under the circumstances, they would become cheats and liars which, if they were caught out, would be held against them with the threat of cancelling all future contracts unless they complied with the process control requirements.

When Hans made me aware of this dilemma, I informed him that I would get to the bottom of this with a concept of "Process Control by Specification Limits", which allowed you to use the charts without sacrificing the tolerance. (and profit)

I then wrote a paper on the subject with formulas, sample charts and their application to the various machining processes in the industry, which was flatly rejected by the automotive industry who was unable to get its head out of the sand.

Who is this fellow Hans Strichow anyway, they asked, as they had never heard of me, upon which I got together with John Bailey at

Bosch Australia (also a client of Hans) who was renowned for his statistical background and expertise.

And when John couldn't fault my paper and solution to the problem in hand, the industry finally agreed to meet Hans and me at his factory where we convinced them that my approach was going to save them money and eliminate the lies.

Hans then got into his head that I had the ability to pull the wool over the customer's eyes whenever he felt like doing so, as he informed me one day when he instructed me to tell lies, simply because he paid me to do so.

He obviously didn't know that I was not for sale, which I told him there and then, which he didn't really understand as his value system was entirely based on the accumulation of money and material possessions.

I didn't work for Hans after that, as I was tired of his weird ways, one of which was his incessant desire to make me feel small in comparison to his accumulated wealth, which he constantly referred to until his untimely death.

I learned about his death when his son rang and informed me that his father was lost at sea, and the only trace they had of him was his big boat which was found miles off shore burnt to a shell without a sign of good old Hans.

His son then asked me whether I was prepared to help him if and when required, to which I agreed, knowing him to be totally different to his father and also very capable of continuing the thriving business his father had built up.

This was not the only time I had terminated a contract, much of which had to do with the attitude of the person at the helm of the business, which was sometimes displayed in the form of a complete lack of control.

At this point, I remind you that my father had frequently lost his control during my life, some of which I have already told you about, and so you will not be surprised to find out that I had developed a sensitivity to this kind of behaviour.

This had made itself known in my role as a parent, as I unable to raise my voice when it came to chastising the children, in which case my wife had to do all the dirty work, whilst I took the easy way out.

Coming back to my clients and the odd screamers, I remember one guy who had little time for cleanliness and order, as you could see in the state of his factory where the dirt had piled up to a crust of an inch or so.

His filing was also atrocious as his desk was piled high with drawings and manuals that made it virtually impossible to find anything, not to mention the quality management system, of which there was none whatsoever.

There was also a distinct atmosphere of 'them and us' between the workers and the two partners, who looked down on their small number of compliant machine operators, which didn't help with my task in hand.

And then the younger boss 'caught' me talking to an operator on a matter of procedure, when he lost his control as he screamed at me like my father used to do at us kids, after which I picked up my case and left – for good.

In doing so, I lost another client who was closely associated with this company where the screamer had spread the news that I was the worst person in the world as I had left them in a lurch, but that didn't bother me.

On another occasion, I had a client who seemed to have a major psychological problem as he never looked me in the eye throughout my dealings with him, where he was the general manager of an international company.

In that context, he was a paid employee who was spending much of his time dabbling in other than work related matters, like selling wine to local restaurants and similar dubious deals, which everybody seemed to know about.

At the same time, he treated his staff with contempt who hated his guts because of this, which created an extremely difficult atmosphere to work in, as I was soon to find out when I tried to train the people in the quality procedures.

I also learned that the majority of the people were just biding their time as they were looking for other jobs or waiting to retire, neither of which constituted a fertile ground for the implementation of a quality management system.

When I informed the boss of my concerns, he also lost his control to the point where he was shaking uncontrollably, as he informed me that this had nothing to do with my contract, and I should concentrate on that and nothing else.

Well, here we go again, as I picked up my case and proceeded to walk out the door, upon which he demanded a refund for his payments thus far, and I couldn't help myself giving him the 'one-finger salute' – good riddens.

Apart from a handful of clients, I was now making my living from Heinz who was my bread and butter customer, as well as the odd sale of my manual, which always gave me a boost in my finances, and so I was happy.

In the meantime, Heinz got his Certificate of Compliance to the ISO 9002 International Standards, after which he needed a part time quality manager, record keeper and process control planner, which I was happy to take on.

I also had another client who deserves a mention, as my relationship with the company was preceded by a meeting with the CEO who informed me that his general manager and brother was a nutcase who needed special treatment.

One of his peculiarities was the fact that he would scream at his employees without warning and for no reason, which I assured him that this was not a problem for me as I had been here many times before – what a lie.

Anyway, he suggested that we meet over dinner so that I could strike up a working relationship with his brother over a drink or two, which we did, and everything seemed to be going quite smooth as we got on well.

Strangely enough, I was suddenly able to contain myself whenever he started to scream at me for no reason, which must have had to do with my forewarning of the possibility, and so I was prepared as I simply told him to "Bugger Off".

Under the circumstances, I didn't have to fear the CEO who had given me a free hand to do as I saw fit, nor did I have to fear his strange brother who seemed to respect me all the more for my ability to stand up to his weird behaviour.

It was then that I looked back on my experiences with the bosses I had encountered in my life so far with respect to some of the weird and wonderful strategies relating to the management of the human resources.

And whilst there were many instances where the boss was considering the human resources as the most valuable asset of the company, the negative experiences seemed to stick in my mind as I recall:

a) One boss who was informing me that he was using the "FIFO" system, which stood for "Fit In or Fuck Off", which seemed to work for him as he had surrounded himself with a bunch of "Yes-men", which is one way to run a business.

At the same time, he had lost a number of really good people, some of which had combined their resources and expertise to start up in competition, which he deemed to be a sign of their evil intent and lack of loyalty to him.

b) Another boss told me that he would get down into the factory and yell and scream at the employees in a random fashion, for no reason other than "To Stir the Pot", as he put it, which did nothing for the morale of the people.

And when it was my turn to get the top managers to carry out the necessary action points, they duly ignored me, and so I yelled and screamed at them as I informed them of my need "To Stir the Pot", and that is when they fired me.

c) On another occasion, I wanted to find out about the boss' investment strategy in the human resource as I asked him whether he would be prepared to give his workers $5 back if they were giving him $10, to which he said "No".

When I inquired about his motivation for the seemingly irrational investment strategy, he replied that they were a lazy pack of bastards that couldn't be trusted, and so they didn't deserve any more that they were getting now.

d) And there is more to come, as I recall this particular company that was generally regarded as "The Revolving Door" within the industry, considering nobody had ever worked for the company for more than three to six months.

When I inquired about the strategy and benefits associated with the brief time of employment and the high training cost, I was informed that they were pushing their employees until they burnt out – which was usually 3 to 6 months.

At the same time, I had come across many bosses who were genuinely interested in the wellbeing of their employees who they considered as the single greatest asset to the business and its sustainability in the long term.

On that note, let me give you my satirical impression of my negative experiences, which is not to condemn the symptom bearers, but rather to put a light hearted spin on "The Worst Case Scenario", as illustrated below.

The Worst Case Scenario

Fig.: 1

In order to overcome the problem, some bosses had developed a bonus system for the gifted employees, who were in the minority, nevertheless, and so the rest simply couldn't care less about the incentive.

And whilst the system worked in isolation, others were affected by the overall performance of the business, which left them to their natural talents and cunning, as illustrated under "The Sales & Marketing Manager".

The Sales & Marketing Manager

Fig.: 2

Some of the other employees had their own way of coping with the situation as they treated the boss with the contempt he deserved, as illustrated below under "The Trouble Shooter".

The Trouble Shooter

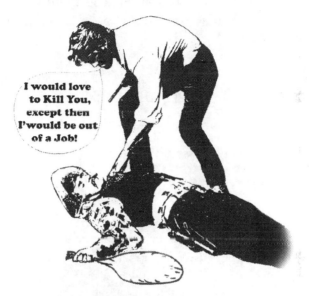

Fig.: 3

That is, some of the more experience members of the staff were asked to engineer their own redundancy, the outcome of which led to their keeping the problems alive until they could leave on their own terms.

Others were unperturbed by all the goings on as they had developed an attitude of self preservation that allowed them to thrive in any kind of positive or negative situation, as illustrated under "The Opportunist".

The Opportunist

Fig.: 4

And then there is always the "The Pessimist" who, by his own inaction and lack of support for the communal good, was creating a self fulfilling prophecy as he claims that he is always right, which he was, as illustrated below.

The Pessimist

Fig.: 5

This is balanced by the production manager who believed in motivating his people with impossible goals in the hope that they will do their utmost to achieve them, as illustrated below under "The Optimist".

The Optimist

Fig.: 6

The quality manager was getting frustrated as he was facing a growing number of complaints relating to the quality of the product, and so he vented his frustration on "The Human Spirit", as illustrated below.

The Human Spirit

Fig.: 7

As the problems began to emerge on the 'Bottom Line', the boss wanted to know what was going on, upon which the general manager told him something about "The Winds of Time", as illustrated below.

The Winds of Time

Fig.: 8

Others remained unaffected by the general turmoil surrounding them on a daily basis as they stuck their head in the sand and pretended that everything was fine with the world, as illustrated under "The Ostrich"

The Ostrich

Fig.: 9

Every so often the boss tried to pull the wool over the seemingly simple minded workers, but this didn't fool "The Skeptic" who had been around long enough to know what's going on, as illustrated below

The Skeptic

Fig.: 10

And then there is "The Philosopher" who seems to have an answer for everything as he surrounds himself with a myriad of toys and perceptions of reality relating to 'The Meaning of Life', as illustrated below.

The Philosopher

Fig.: 11

Thank God "The Powers That Be" were on the ball as they spouted forth their wisdom about "The Winds of Time" with a message that may not have pleased everybody, but then again, it didn't hurt anybody either, as illustrated below.

The Powers That Be

Fig.: 12

This brings me to my aspirations as a doer and my desire to develop a system that was inherently able to create a condition in which all competing influences are balanced, or "Equilibrium", as illustrated below.

The Solution Seeker

Fig.: 13

In the process, I developed a generic "TOP Management Manual", where TOP stands for "Total Organization Performance", which is covering the business process and human resources, as illustrated below.

Total Organization Performance

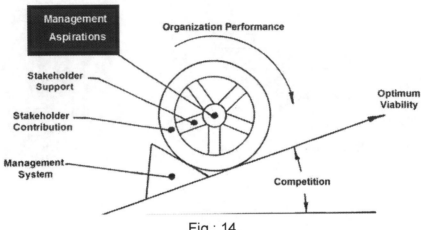

Fig.: 14

The illustration is portraying the relationship between the stakeholders of the business representing the customer, supplier, employee, shareholder and the community at large, and the 'Organization Performance'.

In that context, "The Management Aspirations" would have to be associated with the social role and ultimate purpose of the businesses of industry or needs and expectations of the stakeholders, as illustrated below.

The Management Aspirations

"*The purpose of our business is to create products and services for which there is a demand in the chosen market, the continuity of which is based on our commitment to marketing and innovation.*

In order to do so, the business needs the support of its stakeholders if it is to survive in the short and long term, whereby the future depends on its 'Mutual Appreciation and Performance Standards'.

'Mutual Appreciation' equates to the needs of the stakeholders being catered for by the business, and vice versa, where the 'Performance Standards' reflect the minimum expectations of either party.

The resulting 'Team Spirit' and 'Team Effort' are deemed to produce an ever increasing 'Quality of Life' for the customer, supplier, employee, shareholder and the community as the stakeholders of a thriving business."

Fig.: 15

As to my generic "TOP Management Manual", the initial establishment of a management system was followed by the ongoing development of the inherent potential associated with the human resources and the business process.

And if you think I was on another winner and about to make a fortune from my selling the manuals, you would be wrong, the reason for which was due to the simple fact that I was too far ahead of the Australian market at the time.

To be specific, I was asking the management of the business to make itself accountable to its stakeholders, one and all, and not just the shareholders, which went right against the grain of many a CEO, as I had found out earlier.

The root of the problem had to do with the misperception of reality relating to the purpose of any business, which is to function in a manner that is not unlike the organs in our body, as illustrated below under "The Social Organ".

The Social Organ

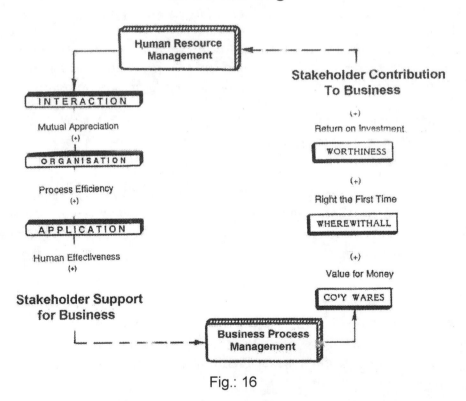

Fig.: 16

In that context, our physical fitness works in an anticlockwise direction resulting in the cells' support for the body, which can then be deployed towards our pursuit of happiness and sustainability in the short and long term.

As it stands, many a business of industry is working in the reverse order to our body, as we can see in its focusing on the 'Return on Investment' first and foremost, which is then followed by its investment in the 'Wherewithal'.

The focus continues in a clockwise direction as the business applies itself to the markets in which it is bound to make a profit, which is followed by its focus on the human effectiveness, process efficiency and mutual appreciation.

In the process, the business may place the pursuit of profit before the needs and expectations of its stakeholders, who may then withdraw their support for the business, as illustrated below under "The Negative Cycle".

The Negative Cycle

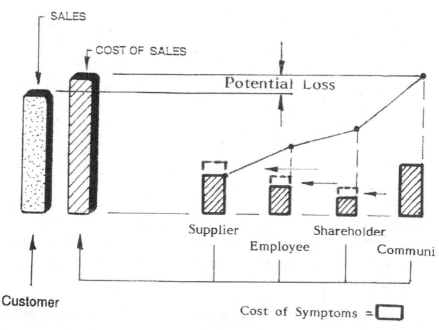

Fig.: 17

Under the circumstances, the community may have to carry the cost of the symptoms, which are then handed back to the businesses and the stakeholders alike in the form of direct and indirect taxes, and so the cycle continues.

On the other hand, other businesses may focus on the stakeholders first and foremost and thus engage in an anticlockwise cycle, where the focus is on the potential gains, as illustrated below under "The Positive Cycle".

The Positive Cycle

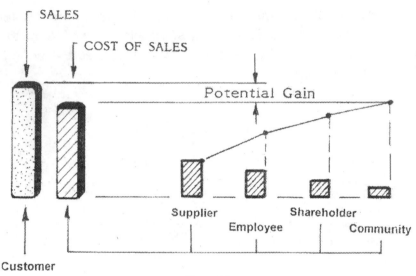

Fig.: 18

Note: The illustrations are an excerpt from the "TOP Management Manual".

In view of my inability to promote the "TOP Management Manual", I wasn't sure whether I still had something to give, or whether I was too far ahead of the time, either way, I would have come to the end of my tether.

And so I thought it might be a good idea to semi-retire whilst continuing my part time job with Heinz and the odd sale of my system, which gave me plenty of time to think about my life and what else there might be for me to do.

It wasn't long before I got bored and looking for something to do, when my rear neighbour Nile chatted to me on the subject of his hedge, which needed trimming badly, and so I offered to do it for him.

As he offered to pay me and I knew him to be filthy rich, I accepted and got on with the job, which I finished much to his satisfaction as we developed a kind of weird and wonderful friendship which I need to tell you about.

It so happened, he was an Arab who had grown up in Kuwait where his parents were stinking rich, which was starting to become a bit of a problem when Kuwait became a hotspot in the Middle East and he decided to get out.

In the process, he bought the house behind us, where he added an indoor pool and generally converted the interior in line with the Arab culture with gold ornaments and fancy furniture and what nots all over the place – each to his own.

He then pointed to his curved driveway and the need to grow a low hedge along the concrete path, like an English box hedge or similar, which he and I went to investigate with respect to the absolute cheapest product in Melbourne.

He ended up buying some sort of fast growing box hedge substitute that looked cheap and nasty, which seemed to be right up his street, as he bought a few hundred of the little fellows which we then proceeded to plant.

As he was an Arab who was basically raised in the desert in an air-conditioned building with no grass or trees in sight, he had absolutely no idea about growing plants and the speed that the plant might then grow at from there.

And so he came rushing over the next day and complained that he had been cheated because the plants had not grown any taller, despite the claim that they were a fast growing variety, which made me laugh out loud.

And whilst this might have been funny for me at the time, I was not amused to find out he would always underpay me and never have any money on him when we went for a coffee, which we did fairly frequently.

On one of these occasions he was casually telling me about his holiday on Hayman Island which happened to be for sale at the time, and so he put in a bid for $164,000,000 dollars whilst I was left to pay for the bill, once again.

If you asked me why I was putting up with this sort of 'friendship', all I can say is that I was intrigued by his personality disorder, some of which I was made aware of by his wife Linda, who he married in England as a student.

She was telling me about their separation, as she couldn't put up with his weird behaviour like when they went to a fancy restaurant and he was looking for a way to get out paying the bill by creating a terrible scene.

He would do similar acts of outrageous behaviour whenever they went to a parent and teacher meeting, a party or any other function where he took the opportunity to make a complete arsehole out of himself.

I told her that I had witnessed this when we went to a small tobacco shop where he was always buying his cigarettes and on this occasion accused the vendor that he was never giving him freebies, or discounts.

And when the poor man explained to him that he was barely making a living, he abused the man to the point where the poor fellow started to tremble and cry, whilst a crowd of people began to gather around us.

In the meantime, he had two Ferraris in his garage, owned three villas worth over two million dollars each, a number of other houses and properties in the Dandenong and also near Sydney, and that is only what I knew.

He also owned a number of factories and a nappy manufacturing business where he had been asked to leave the board of directors as he was an embarrassment to the company which he owned outright.

His wife was living by herself in a magnificent mansion, where she bored herself silly until she discovered that the people at Crown Casino loved her, (for her money) where she spent many a night with her cheap girlfriend.

In doing so, she was giving her girlfriend thousands of dollars to be her friend, whilst she spent the family savings of a cool two million dollars, and when that was gone, so was the red carpet treatment by the Casino.

Now, who would walk away from such an unusual family and a 'friendship' that would make a psychologist's heart sing – out of tune most of the time, as I was to find out.

On that note, let me tell you about the enormous rock out the front of his property which seemed to annoy him, and so I suggested we take it on as a challenge, as we were an unstoppable force together – what the?

And with that, I explained my plan which was to hire a skip and place it next to the rock, after which we would place a sling around the rock and then connect the sling to a torque wrench system that would then pull the rock onto the skip.

However, before we did anything, I wanted to establish how deep the rock was anchored into the ground, for which I attached the sling to my towbar whilst the rear wheels were backed against the curb for extra traction.

In the process, my car was half way across the road as I was attempting to move the rock with an intermittent acceleration, which attracted a bit of an audience, most of which told me that I was a bloody idiot, and I admitted to be.

Anyway, after a little while the rock did finally move a little, which gave me the confidence to continue with the challenge, as I informed Nile that he owed me a glass of beer if I managed to get the rock onto the skip.

You haven't got a chance in hell, he said whilst he nevertheless ordered the skip and the necessary gear, for which he paid out of his own pocket where there had never been any money before – how strange.

Cut a long story short, I did manage to get the rock onto the skip, but I am still waiting for the glass of beer for which he is saving up, I'm sure.

Soon after that I told Nile that I didn't want to continue with our friendship, as I was getting tired of being treated the way he did, which surprised him as he seemed to enjoy our little get togethers where I always paid for everything.

And so I told him straight to the face that he didn't know what friendship was all about as I quoted the number of times when he had taken advantage of me, which seemed to floor him as he had no idea about his wrongdoings.

At the same time, he asked me to teach him how to be a friend and be fulfilled, as he was obviously not happy with his life, much of which had to do with his upbringing in Kuwait were friendship seemed to equate to a monetary pursuit.

"OK, I am willing to give it another go providing you pay me the money you owe me from short changing 'my' pay, going out in 'my' car whilst 'I' paid for the food and the drinks and, last but not least, the glass of beer you still owe me".

And that is when he lost his cool as he informed me that he owed me nothing, whilst he found some excuse why I hadn't really won the bet with the rock, and I was obviously only after his money, after which we never saw each other again.

I felt sorry for him, as he had become the victim of an upbringing that was so intent on pursuing material values that the real values, the things that are for free like my friendship and the love of his wife and kids, had gone out the window.

I also felt sorry for 'The One Pound at a Time Boss', 'The Arsehole from Hell', 'The Penny Pincher', 'The Greedy Quality Management Consultant' and the 'Computer Consultant and his father' who were now rotting in jail.

To all intents and purposes, "The degree of their problems at any one time was proportionate to the perception of reality by one and all", in which case 'they' obviously didn't have a problem, whilst everybody else did.

At the same time, the community is paying for the problems in more ways than one, in which lies an opportunity or two for the solution seekers of this world, as they duly apply themselves to "Our Ultimate Purpose in Life".

Part 3

LIFE IS ALL ABOUT "FULFILMENT"

This brings me to my own perception of reality and the decision to pull out of active service and retire—for good, considering I was now in my late sixties and still able to travel and enjoy life and the fruits of my labour

I suggested to Marion that we should visit Europe for an extensive holiday and experience the cultural diversity by buying an old VW Campervan which would take us wherever we wanted to go, and stay for as long as we liked.

She agreed, and so we set off on our adventure where we visited Germany after having picked up the van in Utrecht in Holland and fitting it out with bedding and whatever else was needed for our trip around Europe.

We started off by visiting my girl cousin in Bremen, who lived out of town in a thatched roof farm house, where she and her husband had retired to after her husband was deemed unfit for driving a car after a head-on collision.

He was still running his legal firm where his wife, Monika, was doing most of the leg work, which left them reasonably comfortable and to enjoy life, whilst being restricted to the public transport system, nevertheless.

Not that her husband was physically unable to drive, but rather mentally unwilling or unable to get back behind the wheel, but they had accepted this as they welcomed us with open arms and the offer to stay for as long as we wanted.

When we told them about our plan to travel all over Europe, they were shocked to the core as they foretold that we would suffer irreparable damage by doing so, much of which had to do with the fact that they had never left Germany.

My cousin was promoting herself as a spiritual animal healer, which we demonstrated to me one day as she waved this crystal over the picture of a horse, which apparently had been sick for a while, and been given up by the local vet.

She then paused as she jubilantly looked at me and explained the irrefutable fact that the horse needed the colour purple, which was obvious to me like the rest of the bull shit she had surrounded herself with.

With that, she equipped herself with a piece of purple cardboard before visiting the unsuspecting horse which must have been so overwhelmed that it died there and then on the spot. (killed itself laughing, I guess)

The next day, I met up with old friends including Klaus, who had been pursuing the dollar in his father's business at the expense of his family and some of his associates who he owed money as he declared himself bankrupt.

He had also sold his car and villa in Spain, which left him with his parental home where he was now in the process of removing his second wife of some 30 years from the premises without leaving her any money whatsoever.

In the meantime, he was living with his wife's sister in law who was much younger than him and had two small children which he now had to care for, which seemed to be keeping him young and sexually active, unlike his ex.

I had a feeling that there was more to the story, as he had inherited a small fortune, some of which went to his first wife who had married him for his money, after which he got smart as he married his second wife with a prenuptial.

The poor girl told us of her plight when we met her clearing her belongings out of the house, without knowing where to go or any money to rent, as the prenuptial wasn't giving her anything if they were ever to split or get a divorce.

Thereafter, I arranged to meet with Klaus at Herman's place, another friend of ours who lived in his inherited house on his own, which he had refurbished immaculately as a bachelor who was also keen on gardening, like Marion.

On the day, I arrived at Herman's before Klaus, which gave me the opportunity to catch up on old times, during which I eluded to my conviction that there must be more to retirement than to put your feet up and wait for God.

He asked me what in the hell I was talking about, and when I mentioned something about his fulfilment as a successful carpenter who was renowned for his professionalism and expertise in building circular stairways, he looked at me strangely.

And with that, he grabbed the phone and rang Klaus who was on his way as he urged him to hurry because I was asking strange questions to which he did not have an answer, which seemed to make him visibly uncomfortable.

"What do you mean by fulfilment?" he said as he pointed to his house, garden and the fact that he was free to do as he saw fit, which was to stay at home and relax and have his girlfriend come over once in a while – what more is there?

I suggested that he might want to write a book about his life as a master carpenter and pass some of his knowledge onto the new generation, or do some research or similar brain activity, which really seemed to unsettle him.

And then Klaus arrived with a few bottles of beer, which immediately changed the atmosphere as we were now surrendering our brains to the pleasures of life, instead of getting all confused by things that obviously didn't matter.

When I tried to make a contribution by wanting to talk about my life in Australia, I couldn't get any interest as Klaus and Herman were too busy discussing the local news and the troubles of the world until we were too drunk to think clearly.

We all agreed that a wonderful time was had by all, and the shame that we couldn't do this more often, considering I was going back to Austria or Australia – Ahhh, who cares, lets have another one for the road.

Somehow, I couldn't see myself fitting back into this environment, as I was still chasing my dream or fulfilment in life, which so many people seemed to be missing out on, but then again, this may not be everybody's cup of tea.

Anyway, we soon got on our way as we set off on our journey and desire to visit Prague as our next destination, which took us into Czechoslovakia where we were faced with a disturbing level of poverty right at the border.

That is, the first township we came to was so poor that some families were sending their children onto the street where they posed for the passing traffic in the obvious capacity of an underage prostitute, which really floored us.

From here on, the poverty angle kept on emerging in a myriad if fashions that shook me personally, as I was always under the impression that Europe was looking after the poor and the underprivileged, but then again, I lived in Australia.

Prague was great as we arrived in mid spring when everything was blooming and dressed in a fresh green colour that couldn't fail to cheer us up, whilst we visited the various tourist attractions from the incredible bridges to the castles.

We continued our journey to Austria, Switzerland and Italy, where we visited Lake Como, Venice, Pisa, Pompeii, Capri, Rome, Naples and many more as we worked our way towards the South of France and Spain.

I remember one Friday evening in the North of Italy when we got caught up in a weekend peak hour rush to anywhere in the country, as long as it was out of town and away from the dreaded high rise living that was everywhere.

As we were either stationary or moving at a walking pace, I decided to pull over in a parking bay and wait until the mad rush had subsided, and as we made ourselves comfortable, one after another car pulled over to do the same.

By the same token, they were not waiting for the traffic to subside, but rather for the radiator to cool down or to inspect the semi-detached exhaust pipe or whatever had come to their attention as an abnormal noise or symptom.

I walked up to the Mercedes with the exhaust problem to see whether I could help, knowing fair well that the average Italian motorist wouldn't know the first thing about the basic 'Bush Mechanic' skills of the average Aussie, like me.

There were four of them gesticulating in a foreign (to me) language that seemed to indicate that they knew the problem, but they didn't know the solution, and so I stepped in and offered my help, which was instantly dismissed.

By all accounts, the problem was beyond their and my capability, which they made clear to me with a body language that was unmistakeable, regardless of the nationality of the person, which immediately spurred me on to prove them wrong.

I looked underneath the car and realized that the exhaust system or muffler had broken off at a point where the broken end was digging into the road, whilst it was hanging on by way of two rubber suspension rings that needed to be dealt with.

I had dealt with this sort of thing in the past, and so I went to fetch a screwdriver, which seemed to get them all exited as they were absolutely sure that this could never work as they physically stopped me from getting to the car.

It was then that I remembered the word 'mechanico', which I spouted forth as I pointed to myself, after which the Red Sea parted and Moses walked through to perform one of his miracles, which quickly got them on the road again.

Low and behold, the word got around as I was now approached by a number of frustrated motor car illiterates, most of whom had a boiling radiator and no water, which wasn't a problem as I offered them ours from the van.

And whilst they all wanted to wait until the radiator had stopped boiling, I did the old trick of loosening the cap and letting the steam escape before starting the motor and pouring the cold water into the radiator a little bit at a time.

Mind you, I could have charged for my services and made a few Euro, but I preferred to tell them that I was an Australian, which meant that nothing was too difficult or impossible for us or, to put it correctly, "I was full of bull shit".

As to our camping arrangements, we often stayed in public car parks, back of a petrol station, meadows, forests, national parks, docks, or side of the road and any other place that was unoccupied and seemingly safe to park.

On one occasion we parked in a meadow off the beaten track in Italy when the car wouldn't start the next morning, which we tried to overcome by trying to push-start the van as we rolled down the hill, but to no avail.

Unable to call for assistance, I investigated the chain of mechanical and electrical activities associated with the starter, which led me to the root of the problem in the form of a frayed flexible cable from the battery to the starter motor.

As I didn't have any tools, I suggested that Marion was to turn the key whilst I was holding the cable onto the starter motor, which worked like a treat, and so we were up, up and away as we got back on the road and looked for a garage.

All in all, we visited 17 countries and travelled 25,000 km in less than three months as we followed our noses without any clear travel plan, but then again, this was to be an adventure and not a precise exercise of tourism and agenda.

In Spain, we were just pulling in next to this mobile home on a wharf where we met an interesting fellow who didn't waste any time to introduce himself, and you could smell him from a distance by the alcohol on his breath.

He was sufficiently sober to tell us about his life as a professor in Vienna where he was asked to pay some back taxes, which seemed to irate him to the point where he left the country for good, together with his missus.

From that moment on, he lived by the rules of the road, which allowed him to stay in a public place for a limited time before he had to move on, and on, and on, as he had been doing for a number of years by now.

At the same time, he looked at Marion and suggested that she would be good for a bit of wife swapping, and so he called for his missus so that I could consider the value of the swap – Oh my God, she was sooo ugly.

When I rejected his offer, he pointed out that she had no teeth, in which case she was perfect for a 'Head Job', which repulsed me even further as I thanked him for his generous offer and accepted a glass of wine instead.

Not that I was seriously entertaining the thought of swapping my wife for anyone, unlike my brother who might have been in there like a shot.

I ended up sharing a bottle of his cheap wine in a plastic bottle whilst he chatted to me in a variety of languages until he passed out and I withdrew myself and returned to Marion who was getting a little worried about me.

On the next morning, we couldn't get away quick enough as we made our way to the South of France and Barcelona, where we visited the La Rambla and many of the other places I had been to in my last business trip to Europe.

We then continued our way to the West of Spain where we ended up in Valencia and met a fellow who was parked in a public parking area, whilst he worked in town in order to earn some money so that he could pay his fine.

Apparently, if you had been found guilty of a traffic or similar offence, you were not allowed to leave town until you settled any outstanding fines, which had detained him for a number of weeks whilst his family was waiting for his return.

After that, I was exceedingly careful with my driving as we continued our journey along the Bay of Biscay on our way to Portugal, where we crossed the Pyrenees on a narrow pass that was even too hard and dangerous for the locals.

From there, we zig-zagged our way to Paris, where we stayed next to the river Seine whilst we visited the key attractions, including the Eiffel Tower, which eluded us until I decided to ask one of the locals, who didn't seem to know what I was talking about.

As it happened, the locals got a kick out of pretending not to know anything, especially if you spoke English, as I found out when I used my hands to describe the shape of the Eiffel Tower, which would have surely jogged his memory.

Instead, the silly bugger was rattling on about Pyramids and all sorts of rubbish as he watched me getting more and more frustrated, and so I decided to let him be as we searched the sky-line and eventually found the tower.

We also experienced some of the ways the Frenchies extorted money from their visitors as we sat in the front of a café on the Montmartre strip, where I ordered a beer and a coffee without first inquiring about the price.

I afterwards found out that the prices were determined by how close you sat to the front of the café or restaurant, and if you didn't inquire about the price, the froggy-buggers would charge you double – Viva la France.

A similar concept happened in Porto in Portugal, where we sat in a café overlooking the harbour and ordered two coffees, which were promptly delivered with some cake and chocolate, which we consumed as we praised the local custom.

That was, until we received the bill for the coffee and the rest, which we then understood as a custom of extorting money from the unsuspecting tourists who were not likely to come back in the near future, and so you might as well hit them hard.

Later on somewhere in Belgium, we ordered some coffee when the waiter bought us some cake as well as the coffee, upon which we knowingly told him that we weren't falling for his trick, as we had been here and done this before.

Well, the visibly upset waiter informed us that it was their policy to make the customers welcome beyond all expectations, and that the cake was free – well, you could have knocked us over with a feather, and so we gave him a generous tip.

I somehow had a funny feeling that, if I hadn't objected to the cake, I might have had to pay for it afterwards, in which case he would have been paid directly as part of the bill, or indirectly as part of a generous tip.

For all I knew, the tourist trade was there to be exploited, and if you failed to do so in one way, there was always plan 'B', but then again, I might have been bitten once too often as I was now twice shy and super sensitive.

We went on to cross the English Channel where we met up with our nephew in London, before we moved on to Bath where I had another girl cousin who was married to a professor at the Bath University, where we stayed a couple of days.

We experienced the delights of the Cotswolds before we headed to Ireland, Scotland and back to England, where we encountered a generator problem that was about to put us out of action for good, as we could not get a spare anywhere.

To specific, the generator shaft had a worn bearing that had ceased altogether as is welded itself into the outer shell, and so it was deemed beyond repair according to the local expert who knew all about this type of thing.

Upon further investigation, he also informed us that there was no spare in the whole of England and Germany, to which I replied that I was an Australian to whom nothing was impossible, which didn't impress him at all.

In my desperation, I suggested that I would be allowed into his workshop so that I could prove my 'Bush Mechanic' skills, which he flatly refused on the basis of some Occupational Health and Safety issue, and so that was it.

He was somehow struck by my claim that I could fix something which he had proclaimed as a Mission Impossible, which might have had something to do with the age old competition between the Aussies and the Pomes.

Anyway, he suddenly changed his attitude as he offered to take on the challenge and prove to me that he was not only an 'English Bush Mechanic', but furthermore a gentleman and a scholar as he proceeded to refurbish the generator.

He must have thought that he won the ashes when he handed me the final product with a big grin on his face as if to say, "I was only joking to see what you might do", which reminded of the French and their treatment of the English.

We continued our journey and returned to my home town where Monika and her husband were only too happy to see us, as they had cherished the thought that we would have surely been killed by now – sorry to disappoint you.

When we offered to share our journey with them together with pictures and stories, they politely declined, which reinforced my impression of their limited interest in the rest of the world, and so we concentrated on the food and the beer.

We continued to explore Bremen and parts of Germany before we decided to cut our journey short by a week, as we were missing our life and family in Australia, which required an emergency call to our travel agency in Melbourne.

As we had no means to do so there and then, we asked the lady in a shop whether we could make a toll free call to Australia, to which she replied that she had to get the permission of the boss beforehand, which turned out in the negative.

We continued by contacting four more shops, but to no avail, which seemed odd as the call was free and they didn't have to go out of their way or pay anything, and so I asked to see the boss in the last place which happened to be a bank.

And when I explained our situation to the man, he looked us up and down as if we were trying to rob his bank before he informed us that he didn't know us, and so why should he trust us with his phone system.

He then proceeded to call the toll free number to make sure that it was indeed free, after which he refused our request nevertheless, and so I gave him my impression of the German culture which seemed to have gone to the dogs since my youth.

And when he insisted that he was only trying to help us and I should be thankful, I really lost my cool as I stormed out of the bank whilst calling him a bloody idiot, which he understood to be 'Free of Charge' and thanked me for accordingly.

If I was to sum up our adventure from start to finish, I must admit that I had visions of a harmonious and balanced culture that was leading the world into a better future for all mankind, in which I was bitterly disappointed.

At the same time, the majority of people seemed happy with their life, despite the poverty and deprivation of the basic needs in the countries we visited, some more than others, which affected me in a constructively discontent sort of a manner.

That is, I was not interested in criticising or condemning the current state of affairs, as I was fully aware of the fact that there are no good guys or bad guys, only symptom bearers and problem solvers, in which case I belonged to the latter.

On that note, I must refer to the two types of "Fulfilment", the first of which has to do with our physical dimension and the need to keep the human race going in the quantitative sense, which is ultimately achieved through the birth of a physical child.

The fulfilment is based on the progressive stages of our growth and development, whereby every transition from our gestation to our childhood, adolescence, adulthood and finally our parenthood represents a stepping stone of sorts.

In that context, our fulfilment is based on the satisfaction of our basic needs which, in the absence of a satisfactory level of gratification as per the values manifested in our genes, we are bound to become a symptom bearer to suit.

And whilst this may be adequate for the solution seekers and their desire to provide better products and services so that we may live longer and better when it comes to our existence here on earth, this is hardly going to last forever.

After all, we are only catering for our physical dimension, which is bound to come to an end when the planet earth is no longer deemed habitable, which is also taking us to the pinnacle of our existence, or demise as a human race.

This brings us to the second form of fulfilment and the need to keep the human race going in the qualitative sense, which is ultimately achieved through the birth of a metaphysical child or brainchild and the satisfaction of our interaction needs.

As a consequence, if we have been deprived during any one stage of our gestation, childhood, adolescence, adulthood and parenthood, we are once again bound to become a symptom bearer to suit the afflicted stepping stone.

In the process, not every person is deemed to be fulfilled in one sense or another, or become a solution seeker relating to 'Our Ultimate Purpose in Life' or pursuit of the great unknown so as to advance the human race.

There is another factor that needs to be considered in the context of our fulfilment insomuch that the gestation process and birth of a physical or metaphysical child cannot be delegated or shared with other people, which I found out soon enough.

That is, I had started a number of discussion groups with people who were similarly inclined, but less active when it came to their discontentment with the world, which ended up becoming more of a rampage than a research group.

I then realized that our metaphysical fulfilment is always associated with our idiosyncrasy, madness or obsession with the pursuit of science, like the physical fulfilment is associated with our idiosyncrasy, madness or obsession with sex.

In that context, "The One Pound at a Time Boss", "The Arsehole from Hell", "The Penny Pincher", "The FIFO Boss", "The Pot Stirrer", "The Revolving Door" and "The Screamers" etc. had essentially offered themselves to science.

At the same time, I felt the need for a body of knowledge relating to "The Quality of the Mind", or "Psy-qua-logy" for short, the context of which is essentially outside the realms of psychology, psychiatry, neurology and all the other ' . . . logies'.

In short, the current bodies of knowledge do not start with the proposition of a 'Grand Order of Design' that is then interpreted in terms of "The Human Condition", which leaves them effectively in the middle of nowhere and without a compass.

In that context, we can imagine ourselves in a position where we are given the goal to travel from here to 'somewhere', the nature of which we are not informed of, and so we cannot follow any road signs or other means of direction.

In our ignorance, we are recording the distance we travel during any one day, which we then compare with the rest of the team, all of which happen to be heading in different directions, whilst nobody knows the specified destination.

In doing so, some may be getting further away from the unknown destination, others may be going around in circles and some others may not go anywhere at all, whilst the rest may actually be heading in the right direction, some of the time.

We can imagine the claims of various individuals as they boast about the progress they made at a certain moment in time or day, that is, until we ask them where they are going, and so they inform us that they haven't got a clue.

Closer to home, we may ask the rich and famous with respect to the ultimate purpose of their pursuit of money, to which many of them may also say "What do you mean?" as they proudly inform us of their worldly possessions.

In the process, they are not only depriving themselves of their ultimate fulfilment as a human being, but they are also bound to cause many problems which are then hopefully solved by other people who may want to satisfy 'their' fulfilment needs.

This brings me to 'my' idiosyncrasy, madness or obsession with 'my' fulfilment need and the age old questions of "Who are we as an Individual?" "What are we doing on this Planet?" and "Where are we going as a Human Race?"

That is, after having studied the various religious, secular and scientific interpretations, I came to the conclusion that there was no common perception of reality, as illustrated below under "The History of the Meaning of Life".

The History of the Meaning of Life

a) To realize one's potential and ideals

b) To achieve biological perfection

c) To seek wisdom and knowledge

d) To do good, to do the right thing

e) To meanings relating to religion

f) To love, to feel, to enjoy the act of living:

g) To have power, to be better

h) To life having no meaning

i) To know and understand the meaning of life

j) To the perception that 'Life is bad'

Fig.: 19

And whilst there have been a large number of proposed answers from many different cultural and ideological backgrounds and speculations throughout history, we are still largely in the dark when it comes to 'Our Ultimate Purpose in Life'.

The reason for this lies in part with the scientific community and its predominant focus on the empirical facts and figures about the physical nature of the universe and the parameters concerning the 'how' of life.

Yet, the answer is more so associated with the 'why' of life and the philosophical and religious conceptions of existence, social ties, consciousness, happiness, value, purpose and the conception of God.

An alternative approach poses the question "What is the meaning of 'my' life?" in which case the purpose of life may coincide with the achievement of an ultimate reality, a feeling of oneness, or even sacredness.

The truth of the matter appears to lie in a combination of both, whereby the human race is not just a collection of individuals pursuing their happiness in isolation, but a 'family of man' that is looking out for each other.

As it stands, this perception of reality has not yet filtered into the minds of the people around the world, the cause of which has to do with the absence of a common vision relating to 'Our Ultimate Purpose in Life'.

Under the circumstances, anybody can claim a mandate, be it related to the individual's pursuit of its own happiness in isolation, with friends and family, the wider community, if not the entire human race.

Not satisfied with my finding, I decided to research the subject from the ground up with respect to the proposition of a 'Grand Order of Design' relating to everything in the universe and its connection to 'The Human Condition'.

My obsession led to my writing a book by the title "Our Ultimate Purpose in Life", in which I describe my findings in a down to earth manner so as to serve as a prerequisite for anybody wishing to apply the 'TOP Management' principles.

As the ultimate intent of the book was "to pursue the great unknown so as to advance the human race", it was written in the form of a reference manual that was specifically aimed at:

a) The seekers of knowledge who are 'constructively discontent' with the scientific communities and/or belief systems and their answers to 'Our Ultimate Purpose in Life', which is leaving them in a moral vacuum.

b) The education, training and consulting facilities who are ultimately responsible for shaping the minds of the up and coming generations with respect to their desire and ability to create a better world for all mankind.

c) The businesses of industry which are left to the process of trial and error when it comes to their obligations as a human organization and commitment to the needs and expectations of the stakeholders, and vice versa.

As to aim c), the objective is based on a separate business manual reflecting my experiences and developments as a management consultant to the businesses of industry, as illustrated below under:

Part 3—The Human Organization:

3.1 Total Organization Performance
3.2 Human Resource Management
3.3 Human Resource Development
3.4 Business Process Management
3.5 Business Process Development

For further information, please contact hansstrichow@yahoo.com.au

The book is reflecting my fun, frustrations and fulfilment in life, the latter of which led to my giving birth to a "Brain Child" that is designed to advance the human race, as shown below.

Our Ultimate Purpose in Life

Contents

And so I have come to the end of my autobiography in the hope that my fun, frustrations and fulfilment in life have provided you with something that is a) worthy of your time, and b) worth following up by reading my other books entitled:

1.—Our Ultimate Purpose in Life

2. – The Human Organization

As to my current commitment to the advancement of the human race, I am running a series of workshops with the "University of the

Third Age", (U3A) where I am having the time of my life, whilst I am watching the world go by.

The Author

Still coming out of his shell – at 72